Pierre-Gabriel GONZALEZ

Bibendum

100 Years
of the Michelin Man
in posters

Michelin
46, avenue de Breteuil - 75324 Paris cedex 07
Tel. 01.45.66.12.34 - 36.15 Michelin - www.michelin.com
Graphic conception: Agence Le Sanglier
Archives: Michelin
Text: Pierre-Gabriel Gonzalez
Translation: Aperto Libro
Layout and photoengraving: Agence Le Sanglier

INTRODUCTION

Descended from the official handbills "plastered" on walls for the public's edification since printing first began, the advertising poster has existed as a double paradox for over a century. Short-lived by definition, it announces an event or presents an object of limited life. Nevertheless, through its layout, colour and the power of its message, the poster and its claims often carry more than a simple piece of promotional information; owing to its creators' talents, it can rise to being a genuine work of art. It often reflects the preoccupations of our modern societies; no doubt this is why it so fascinates us.

Urban centres became more and more densely populated in the late nineteenth century; as a result a well-placed poster, costing mere pennies, was seen by several thousand people daily. As in today's election campaigns, teams with glue-pots competed for the best spots on walls and hoardings. Printers and businessmen called on promisingly talented beginners to create these posters, such as Manet, Chéret, Mucha, Toulouse-Lautrec and many others...

"Street art", although no longer in its youth', still fascinates a hundred years later, despite the development of magazine publishing, the appearance of radio, television, and digital networks. Even if printing techniques (chromolithography, photoengraving, typography, offset), conception and layout of the message have completely changed, the poster still remains a media truly for "the people", reaching out to the general public. Without a doubt it is this "direct" communication, without artifice, which explains its power and its perpetuity.

1898
1998

This immediacy, this possibility to communicate without risking confusion or distortion by the medium, explains the permanence of the poster in Michelin advertising and promotion. Moreover, how could it be otherwise? Hasn't Bibendum (the Michelin Man) always been very much at ease in the street, there where his tyres have been ensuring vehicle mobility for more than a century?

PRESENTATION

The Michelin Man, conceived in 1898 from the imagination of the Michelin brothers and O'Galop's pencil, holds a very special place in the world of international advertising. Today Bibendum is recognised and regarded with tremendous affection on five continents and he is completely identified with the product he has been fashioned with - the pneumatic tyre.

At the turn of the 19th century our grandparents, the Belle Epoque drivers, discovered both the Michelin tyre - which invited them to "drive on air" - and the good-natured fellow or the rubber man whose motto was "drinks up obstacles", to handle the small impediments of the road as easily and smoothly as one would quaff a glass of champagne. They were both just as quickly and unreservedly adopted!

The rubber man was soon christened Bibendum; the rise of the automobile and the advertising genius of the Michelin brothers took care of the rest.

By turn demi-god, defender of great causes, the motorist's guardian angel, travel guide, theatrical character or James Bond's friend, Bibendum has become today a sort of worldwide hero, using his legendary good nature, as well as his competence concerning tyres and the road, to serve all.

Unquestionably, no other company mascot has withstood the voyage through this century so well, a century nevertheless marked by many famous people. Inflated by that most banal and universal element, air, compressed to give him life, he was well brought up by attentive parents. As a herald of endlessly innovative products, Bibendum has also been well served by masterly poster-designers. Drawing immoderately on some fountain of youth, he has always adapted to circumstances with spontaneity and a certain disregard for fashion. Very much a part of his century, he has nevertheless remained unchanged by the vicissitudes of time.

A representative selection

The advertising poster is the medium which brought about Bibendum's birth - his cradle, in a manner of speaking - and it has been his companion throughout a century, everywhere where vehicles are driven. It is therefore the best place for everyone to see him live, move and deliver his message. Such is the reason for this publication.

It could be considered virtually impossible to condense to one volume a hundred years of the Michelin image through advertising posters and through a quasi-omnipresent Bibendum. Indeed, over 3 000 posters have been published by the manufacturer since 1898, not only in Europe, but also in North America, Africa, Asia... and elsewhere!

These 250 posters were therefore chosen with the greatest care, according to three criteria: their representability with regard to Michelin's various publicity campaigns (history, social actions and products); their graphic and aesthetic excellence; and finally, their international character, thus demonstrating the worldwide dimensions of the industrial group and Bibendum himself. This amazing rubber man guides us through the entire selection, giving advice in about twenty different languages - Bibendum is indeed a "man of the world"!

Finally, it should be emphasised that this world anthology of the Michelin poster constitutes a true "event", worthy of Bibendum's hundredth birthday; for the first time the public will see graphic archives which were dispersed and often ignored. The book will become a must for those keen to become better acquainted with the Michelin Man.

Bibendum and the Poster : A Hundred-Year-Old Alliance

It is difficult to date precisely the appearance of the first advertising poster. We know it came into existence at the end of the nineteenth century, shortly before the period when the Michelin brothers and O'Galop chose this medium to present their "Michelin Man" to the public in 1898.

A hundred years later, these two roughly contemporary "creations" - the poster and the Michelin Man - are just as faithful to each other and as popular as ever. Bibendum and the poster have followed this century's ups and downs together, have reflected its changes and are still largely associated with each other in the minds of their friends.

Because of his perpetuity through the decades, because of his omnipresence, Bibendum is undeniably Michelin's corporate messenger. Since 1898 he has been a familiar figure on a large majority of the chosen posters; moreover, when he was absent from the composition, certain Michelin posters were no longer recognised with the same spontaneity.

Nevertheless, Bibendum's mere presence on the poster does not in itself make an interesting graphic art style; but he is worthy of study because he is a character with a thousand facets. Indeed, he is constantly undergoing changes according to the period, the country, the designer's interpretation, sometimes even the message being promoted. Running alongside his tyre he is simply the company trademark while at other times he can be animated with an intangible vitality, as shown in the few "portraits" reproduced in these first pages! There are cases when he is not alone and the multiplication of "Bibs" transforms certain posters into lively theatrical scenes!

Another interesting facet: the character's unchanging and brilliant whiteness, so unexpected when evoking a tyre which is generally entirely black; this aspect constitutes a strong identifying feature throughout all Michelin publicity. Upon analysis, the white surface, its average area and its disposition on the poster, may tell us much about Bibendum's promotional impact.

When explaining the centennial relationship between Bibendum and the poster, three main periods can be defined.

❶ A Golden Youth (1898-1924)

The Belle Epoque is the first great period of the poster, when truly great artists took an interest in laying claim to mural work in general. The fever had already overtaken collectors who paid extravagantly for superb chromolithographic creations.

Bibendum, a facetious and pugnacious gentleman.

The first Michelin posters largely reflect the humour which is characteristic of the 1900s. Elements of sport, poetry, and general culture are found together with allusions to Greek and Roman mythology and theatrical events of the moment.

Bibendum, the very incarnation of the tyre and a combative and emblematic character, adapts to his public in terms of his "dress" as well as his behaviour. Varying with the imagination of his illustrators, he is seen wearing spectacles or a monocle, laced boots or cyclist's shoes; he sports cuff-links and a signet-ring, and constantly smokes a respectably large cigar.

This first generation Bibendum is at the same time a joyful companion and a fighter, who likes to play tricks on his competitors and who excels at making his friends and customers laugh.

The message

Bibendum is entrusted with several "missions": to establish the supremacy of the pneumatic tyre over the solid one; to present Michelin products to their best advantage; and to compete for the triumph of his colours throughout Europe, and from 1908, in North America.

"The Michelin tyre drinks up obstacles", the first of the claims made for the new product, implies a clear superiority owing to the "air cushion"; it also means the superiority of the brand; it is, in short, the birth certificate of the modern automobile.

The "Semelle" or "Sole" tyre, reinforced with metal studs (1905), provides protection against punctures; another message appears widely to promote the bicycle tyre: "the best, the least expensive". Here already is the sales argument of low prices, which is later to become that of money saved due to the longevity of the product itself.

After the First World War the automobile becomes accessible to a wider public (this is the period of the "Cable", then the "Confort" tyre), which naturally leads Bibendum to be unsparing with advice for his customers on how to inflate and maintain tyres.

Aesthetics

As the advertising poster is meant to promote a product, it must be straightforward and without fancy embellishments. Therefore, Art Nouveau and its dreamlike women largely do not figure on the Michelin poster, with the exception of A. Renault's creation which tends instead to be closer to Bouisset's realisations for Chocolat Menier (1892) or those of Vavasseur for Ripolin paints (1898). Generally speaking, the Michelin poster presents simple graphic ideas, rather than expressing elaborate artistic compositions far removed from the serious message of tyre quality.

The artists

Most Michelin posters, corresponding with the practice of the period, are commissioned from illustrators, such as Poulbot, Fabiano, Cousyn, Vincent, Montaut...

Marius Rossillon, alias O'Galop, Bibendum's first designer, holds a special place in that he gives life to the character and his activities over a period of about fifteen years (with the exerciser, the "Semelle" tyre, the bicycle tyre, etc.)

It is interesting to note that these artists, in their Bibendum period, are often little more than beginners. Without a doubt, the Michelin brothers remembered their own years of study (about 1870-75) at the Ecole des Beaux-Arts, the famous Parisian fine arts school, and were therefore familiar with certain artistic circles and young talents.

Aside from these creators, recognised trailblazers in the history of advertising art, other names should be cited: Philibert, Genevrier (known as the "Grand Aigle", or Great Eagle), Hindre, Renault, Roowles, etc. Less well-known to the public at large, they nevertheless brought to life Bibendum, each in his own way, marking him with a particular style of drawing or a characteristic trait.

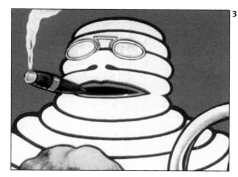

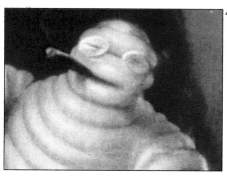

1 - O'Galop (page 155, no 9)
2 - René Vincent (page 128, no 1)
3 - Fabien Fabiano (page 126, no 2)
4 - Albert Philibert (page 125)

❷ Still "drinking up obstacles" (1925-1986)

Although favoured by a certain expansion in the 1920s and 1930s, the poster, a medium appreciated by the public, is rapidly challenged by the press, cinema, radio, and later, television.

The French poster artists Loupot, Colin and Cassandre bring Cubist and Art Deco influences to poster production. Elaborate text and photomontage both become integral parts of the design.

Metamorphosing Bibendum

The birth of the best-known Bibendum comes in 1925 with the arrival of a much wider tyre, the "Comfort". The drawing is simplified by reducing the number of tyres composing his arms, legs and torso. The subsequent outline of the character was not to change significantly until our own period. The loss of the cigar, however, takes place about 1929 as part of the firm's efforts to limit the ravages of tuberculosis. In fact, some of his accessories fixed him in time.

At the start of the 1960s, Bibendum goes through a hiatus (doesn't even the sun have eclipses...?). For about twenty years he is no longer present systematically on every poster, he remains "in the wings" of the campaigns, reduced to a small-sized corporate image, even when promoting various sports or technological exploits of the time. For example, the success in "Formula One" or the establishment of a sales base in the United States take place virtually without his services! It should be noted that the tourist publications were able to resist this tendency and maintained a strong relationship between the character and his public.

The message

Over this long period of about sixty years, the advertising message of the trademark has changed, of course, but the sense of direction has remained constant: that of technical progress.

From the 1930s, it is a long way to the "Radial" which starts with the "Superconfort", the "Pilote" and the "Metallic", the first tyre to succeed with a combination of rubber and steel cords.

In 1946, the patent of the "X" tyre gives Bibendum the difficult task of proving the worth of a new tyre structure by means of a highly technical demonstration, and this in spite of delaying tactics by certain competitors and car makers. This is the "period of glory" with Bibendum mobilised into promoting the radial and the setting up of factories in the principal world markets. The successive generations of the "X" ("XAS", 1965; "ZX", 1967; "XZX", 1975, etc.) are therefore accompanied by great advertising campaigns where the poster was predominant.

Aesthetics

The first photomontages appeared on Michelin posters about 1925: this very modern, image-oriented technique is often counterbalanced by Bibendum's presence, whose simple lines always integrate perfectly. Up until about 1985 the coexistence of Bibendum and photography creates a certain permanence in the Michelin poster style.

The creation

After André Michelin's death (1931), few posters are signed by independent artists. It is now the Parisian in-house advertising department (Michelin Paris Studio) which assumes responsibility for poster creation, alternating between a strict respect for the traditional rules of graphic art and a few audacious initiatives.

For several decades the Michelin Paris Studio breathed life into the firm's advertising, creating a great number of remarkable works worthy of museums and international collections. On a few occasions, Raymond Savignac, a master of the contemporary poster, joined forces with the team of in-house graphic artists to work for Bibendum.

1 - "Snow Tyre", (page 99, no 1)
2 - "Red Guide", (page 86, no 1)
3 - "New "XAS"", Savignac (page 85, no 6)
4 - "World Championship", (page 76, no 1)
5 - "Baby Campaign", (page 24, no 1)

❸ "Everyone on Michelin" (since 1986)

Since the mid-1980s, Michelin advertising campaigns have been conceived on the basis of continents, with variations specific to each country.

The spread of television changed the world of communication, however the poster held its ground - omnipresent and permanent, but now with dimensions (4 x 3m or more) which would have made O'Galop grow pale! In contrast to the fugitive images of the new media, the poster alone is present where the motorist makes his or her choice and places an order. It is still a common feature of today's world.

The message

It was the "Everyone on Michelin" campaign launched by the BDDP agency in 1986 which repositioned Bibendum as the standard-bearer, as much for the customers as for the Group's own employees.

Today, several agencies and the Paris Studio direct Michelin advertising, putting the accent on technological arguments and product innovations as well as developing Bibendum's constant concern for the preservation of the environment ("Energy" campaigns).

Bibendum returns, therefore, more than ever as Michelin's chief messenger. He confirms the industrial group's worldwide calling and at the same time returns to the theme he has cherished for three quarters of a century: that of a tyre, round like our planet and fitting all types of vehicles, even the space shuttle!

Today, for his hundredth birthday, the new Bibendum "look" marks a twofold care for tradition and progress; a dynamic and slimmer Michelin Man, younger than ever, is ready to face the challenges of the twenty-first century.

Back to the future

The reader is now invited to travel back in time, from the most recent campaigns to the beginnings of the tyre in the French Auvergne, a hundred years ago...

Throughout these pages, presented in reverse chronological order and with Bibendum for a travel companion, the reader will discover Michelin's great advertising themes, the variety of products and all the initiatives the firm has taken in the service of Man's mobility. Some posters recall the special contribution of Maps and Guides to the development of tourism and motoring.

To make it easier to place dates, each of the sixty "chapters" begins with an indication of the period during which the posters illustrated appeared.

Have a good trip back through our century, now coming to a close. May Bibendum guide you on your way...

Pierre-Gabriel Gonzalez
8 December 1997

1 - "Bibendum running with tyre", 1925 (page 114, no 1)
2 - "MX tyre", 1980 (page 37, no 6)
3 - "Three hundred ways of saying Tyre", 1986 (page 40, no 2)
4 - "Bibendum in space", 1994 (page 11, no 1)

Bibendum Tops
the Bill

This Thai poster very much emphasises Bibendum's modernity. Since his birth a hundred years ago, he has always been ready to get our planet on the move, and, if necessary, to travel in space. In the lower part of the poster, the Earth shows the company's field of investigation; Michelin's vocation is to equip anything that can be driven on earth.

Thailand 1995
"Michelin's new MXF Club technology
Drive yourself right out of this world"
Language: Thai
Product presented: MXF Club tyre
600 x 900mm

Bibendum in the Celestial Empire

Thursday, 19 December 1996, Shen Yang, Manchuria. A year to the day after the signature of a joint venture creating the Michelin Shen Yang Tire Company Ltd, the first Michelin tyres leave the Chinese factory. In Chinese "19 December" means: "I want to have a child, I want to live for a long time".

①

1 - China 1997 (Hong Kong)
Michelin, MXF Sport. Handles all tight turns, improves road grip at high speeds
Language: Cantonese
297 x 420mm

Fitted out with trainers and in-line skates, Bibendum cannot help but appeal to young drivers.

China, 1996 (Taiwan)
"Michelin, MXT
Evacuates water at a speed
of 2 gallons/second. Drive on
a wet road as if it were dry
Farewell aquaplaning!"
Language: Chinese
297 x 420mm

It should be noted that the advertising claim
for this product was formulated as the
following in Europe: "The tyre that dries
the road". This explains Bibendum's
"sucking" action!

3

China, 1995 (Taiwan)
"Michelin Pilot. The only top-of-the-range
tyre that understands the needs
of today's motorist
CX...HX...SX..."
Language: Chinese
420 x 600mm

A plain poster where Bibendum is featured
as a discrete corporate trademark.

1990
1995

When Japan adopts Bibendum

Bibendum has the advantage of his "sumo wrestler" proportions in appealing to the Japanese; it helps him fit in perfectly in the Land of the Rising Sun, which is modern and traditional at the same time.
The idea of a Bibendum travelling all over the world to deliver his tyres is one of the constants in Michelin advertising.
This Japanese poster from the 1990 campaign suggests the central idea of serving the customer, wherever he or she may be in the world.
More recently, the "MXGS" tyre poster, with its extremely simple layout, takes up the idea again of comparing the round shape of the tyre and the globe. It obtained a first prize in advertising in 1995.
In the 1990 campaign, (posters 3 to 7), a three-dimensional Bibendum presents himself in all his various activities: tyre manufacturing, racing competition and the tourist guides, without forgetting the lesson in how to pronounce the name Michelin in Japanese.

2

MICHELIN

ミシュランは、地球との摩擦を減らしました。

タイヤと路面との摩擦（転がり抵抗）が小さくなれば、その分、燃費は向上し、省エネルギーや公害防止に大きく貢献できます。歴史的にみて、転がり抵抗の低いタイヤの開発は、それほど難しいことではなかったのですが、残念ながら、ウェット路面でのグリップ力やハンドリング、寿命といったタイヤの基本性能の低下を伴わざるをえないものでした。しかし、ミシュランは、グリーンXテクノロジーによって、他の諸性能はまったく損なわずに、転がり抵抗を一段と低減させることに成功しました。このグリーンXテクノロジーを日本で最初に導入したのがミシュランのMXGS。転がり抵抗の

大幅な低減を実現させると同時に、ウェット路面でのグリップ力、ハンドリング、静粛性、タイヤの寿命など、卓越した基本性能の確保も両立させたのです。このグリーンXテクノロジーは、ミシュランが打ち立てた最新の技術。1946年にミシュランが開発したラジアルタイヤと同じように、グリーンXタイヤもまた、変わりゆく社会のニーズに対応したものといえます。理想のタイヤを目指した私たちの追究はドライバーにも地球環境にも有益なタイヤを、絶えず作り出していきます。ミシュランのMXGSなら、「地球との摩擦」を減らした快適なドライブが楽しめるというわけです。

MXGS				TYPE:HR
タイヤサイズ	外径(mm)	外幅(mm)	適 合 リ ム	希望小売価格(円)
● 195/60R15 88H	204	824	5½'-6-6½'-7	35,200
205/60R15 91H	211	837	5½'-6-6½'-7-7½	37,200
● 215/60R15 94H	216	839	6'-6½'-7-7½	39,200
● 195/65R14 89H	204	820	5½'-6-6½'-7	24,900
195/65R15 91H	204	845	5½'-6-6½'-7	27,600
205/65R15 94H	211	858	5½'-6-6½'-7-7½	30,100
215/65R15 96H	225	872	6'-6½'-7-7½	33,000

＊は計測サイズです。各サイズともチューブレスタイプです。
＊印のサイズは発売予定サイズです。

■希望小売価格はタイヤ本体の価格であり、税者料、入替料、バランス調整料などの整備料金は含まれておりません。■使用済みのタイヤを処理するには費用がかかっております。
■当カタログ記載の希望小売価格は、販売店が販売する価格を拘束するものではありません。■希望小売価格には、消費税は含まれておりません。

■グリーンタイヤのより詳しい内容は、製品カタログをご参照ください。またはミシュランオカモトタイヤ並びに各販売会社にお問い合せください。

93131100000-A

ミシュランオカモトタイヤ 株式会社
〒102 東京都千代田区九段北2丁目1番6号 TEL.03-3210-2731

1

Japan, 1990
"Michelin manufactures 440 000 tyres
for 110 000 cars"
Language: Japanese
Corporate poster
1 050 x 360mm

2

Japan, 1995
"Michelin reduces friction with the Earth"
Language: Japanese
Product presented: MXGS tyre

3

Japan, 1990
"How do you do?
May I introduce myself: Michelin"
Or the pronunciation of the Michelin name,
for beginners
Language: Japanese and English
Corporate poster
500 x 360mm

④
Japan, 1990
"Michelin is one of the world's leading
tyre manufacturers"
Language: Japanese and English
Corporate poster
500 x 360mm

⑤
Japan, 1990
"Michelin has been making solely tyres for
100 years"
Language: Japanese and English
Corporate poster
500 x 360mm

6

7

Bibendum in Japan

The first business deal with the Japanese goes back to 1964. The company's presence was reinforced in 1978 by the creation of the "Nihon Michelin Tire", a distribution firm which greatly helped in the sale of car tyres. In 1989, the creation of the "Michelin Okamoto Tire Corporation" made it possible to modernise an existing tyre factory in Ohta. Michelin was the first manufacturer and one of the rare Western industrial firms to produce in Japan; the new challenge was to be Japanese in Japan, as Michelin had been able to be American in the United States, British in Great Britain, Italian in Italy, etc. Owing to the quality of his products and customer service, Bibendum is today a member of the very select group of component suppliers to Toyota, Mitsubishi, Subaru and Daihatsu and has obtained the title of "priority supplier" for Honda.

Bibendum goes ecological to save our Planet Earth

To prove his ecological awareness, Bibendum launches a campaign in 1994 to demonstrate the energy savings achieved with the "Energy" tyre.

The ways of expressing the new message are quite different: in the United States, the accent is on stressing the value of science, "that goes beyond magic!" which received awards as one of the ten best American advertising campaigns in 1995; in Europe, Bibendum is omnipresent in the poster campaign, and in Asia the emphasis is on energy economics. It is indeed a new era dawning with the "Energy" tyre: that of promoting greater respect for the environment, the fundamental challenge of the twenty-first century.

The campaign can be summarised as follows: the "Energy" is the tyre of "four times less"

- less resistance,
- less fuel consumption,
- less pollution,
- less expenditure...

On posters 1, 2 and 6, Bibendum has disappeared in favour of the company's ecological message, but he is at the very heart of the "Energy" campaign billed throughout Europe.

Le pneu vert est né en Auvergne

MICHELIN

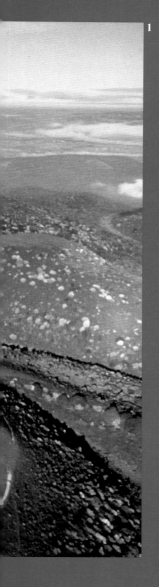

ENERGY MXV4
WITH RADIAL XSE TECHNOLOGY

It's
science
that goes
beyond
magic!

MICHELIN

①
France, 1994
"The Green tyre was born in the Auvergne"
Language: French
Corporate poster: Energy
400 x 600mm
This poster is an illustration of the Auvergne's good fortune at the turn of the century; its harmonious economic development hasn't jeopardised its ecological balance. The "Energy" tyre was developed in the Michelin research centre at Ladoux, near Clermont-Ferrand.

②
United States, 1995
"Energy MXV, with radial XSE technology
It's science that goes beyond magic!"
Language: English
Product presented: MXV4 tyre
510 x 1160mm

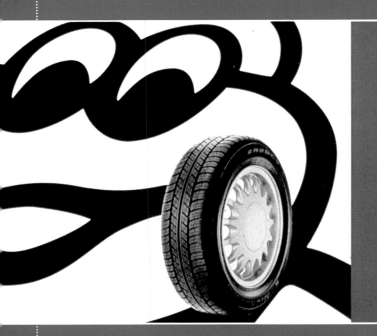

DIE GRÜNE REVOLUTION VON MICHELIN:

ENERGY

MICHELIN

❸

Germany, 1994
"Michelin's green revolution: "Energy"
Language: German
Product presented: "Energy" tyre

❹

Netherlands, 1994
Billboard
"Save 200 litres per 50 000 kms
The new Michelin "Energy"
Less energy to move forward"
Language: Dutch
3000 x 4000mm

❺

Belgium, 1994
"Energy" campaign posters on street
billboards
Language: French
3000 x 4000mm

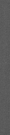

Bibendum-gripping on two wheels

The last vehicle to take advantage of radial tyre technology (in 1987) was the motorbike and it has become a firm favourite with Bibendum. Whether in trial or endurance events, all-terrain or over asphalt, of American, European or Japanese manufacture, the big bikes have taken Bibendum's colours to first place on the podiums each season for about ten years now. On two very creative Japanese posters an invisible motorcycling champion sets down his impressions, as traditional samurais did after combats. A completely different style can be seen in Europe, with two Bibendums in leather jackets seen from behind: one is the "cool" road biker, who would be the type to take his massive motorcycle out for a long easy-going ride; the other is the tense biker hunched over for speed, the bodywork and his boots scraping the asphalt as he makes a tight turn...

1 ....

Europe, 1996
"Just because you drive on the same road doesn't mean that you need the same tyres"
Product presented: Road bike tyre
300 x 420mm

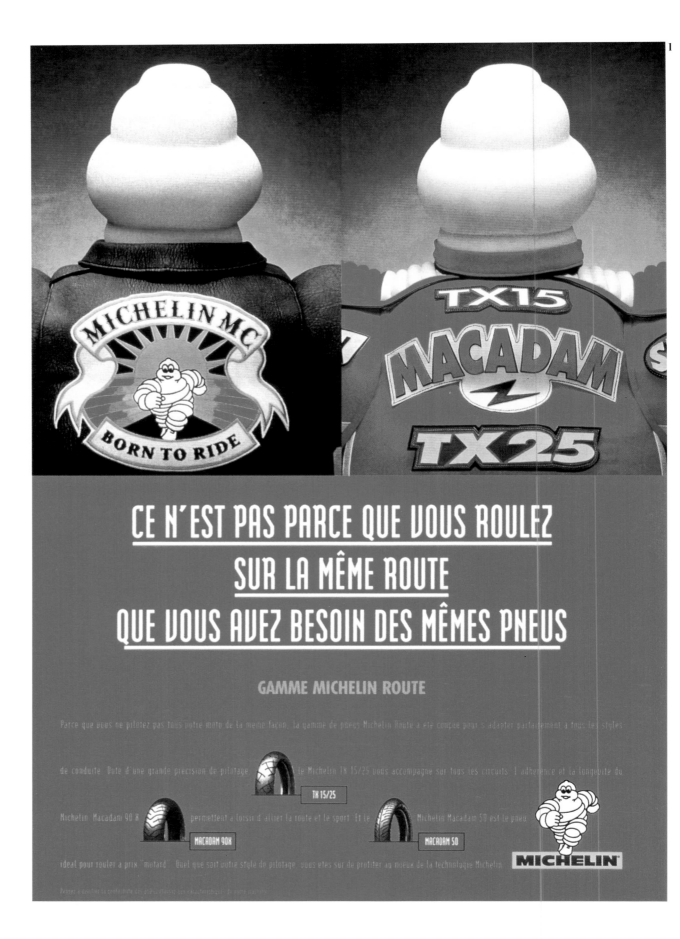

CE N'EST PAS PARCE QUE VOUS ROULEZ SUR LA MÊME ROUTE QUE VOUS AVEZ BESOIN DES MÊMES PNEUS

GAMME MICHELIN ROUTE

2

3

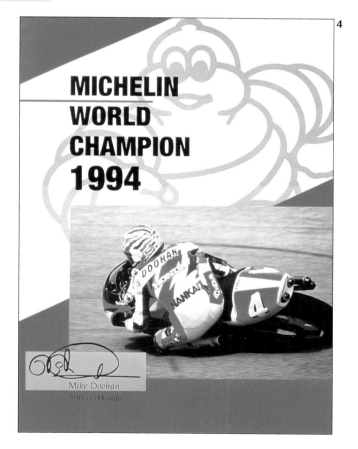

4

Bibendum on two wheels with the throttle wide open

From 1974 to 1997, during the Motorcycle Grand Prix, with all engine sizes from 50cc to 500cc, including the 80, 125, 250 and 350, Bibendum carried off 58 world champion titles. Superbike has taken 6 world champion titles since 1988. In Endurance, 10 titles between 1980 and 1997. Finally, in Trials, Bibendum earned no less than 16 world champion titles between 1981 and 1997.

Bibendum campaigns in North America

The early 1990s are marked by Michelin strengthening its presence on the American continent. The most popular publicity campaigns of these years were those based on those most fragile and precious of beings: babies.

The idea was to make the American public aware of the importance of the family car's tyres and their condition; the second car is the one in which all the family leaves for weekend adventures.

Variations on the baby theme were many; dressed in sou' westers, safe, despite the bad weather; curled up in an "MXV", sleeping peacefully; dressed in chequered nappies (made from a race course victory flag), safe in the knowledge of the reliability of the "EP-X Sport", etc.

To launch this especially popular campaign, a great many TV spots were placed, while the posters played a more modest role on the North American continent. In Australia, on the other hand, the street and road advertising maintained its importance and several "baby" campaign posters won professional prizes. Out of consideration for these babies, Bibendum is only partly visible, discreet and smiling...

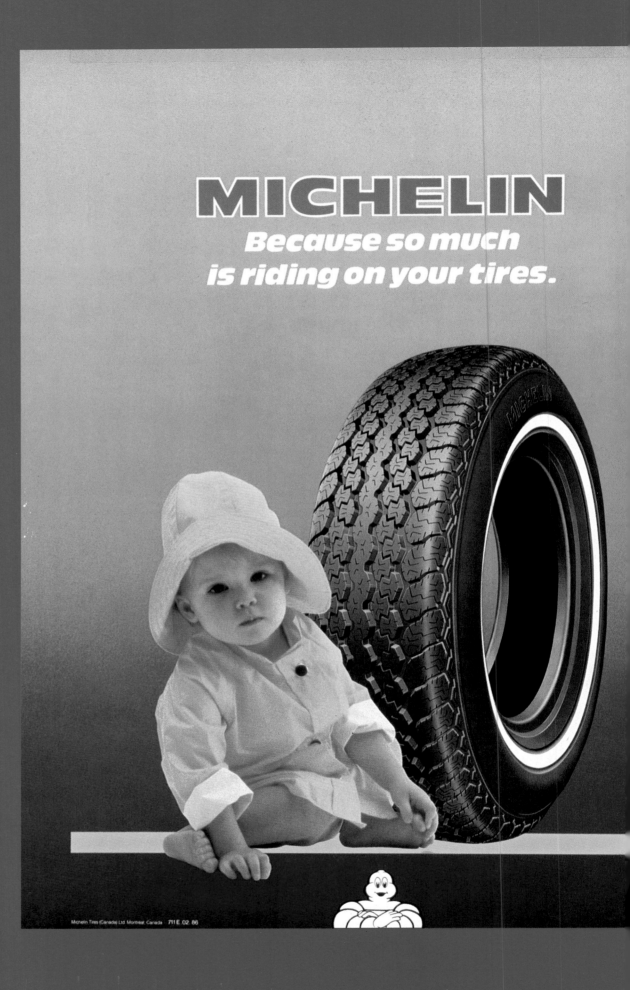

Another safe delivery.
Michelin. Because so much is riding on your tyres.

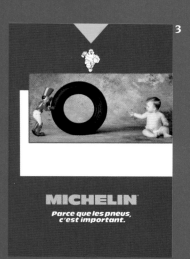

MICHELIN
Parce que les pneus, c'est important.

MICHELIN
Parce que les pneus, c'est important.

SPORT EP-X

Une performance superbe...
toute l'année.

■ Excellente tenue de route, stabilité accrue et bonne réponse du véhicule.

■ Adhérence remarquable sous la pluie et excellentes capacités de traction toutes saisons.

■ Une allure superbe qui rehausse le "look" sportif de votre voiture.

Bibendum in the United States

Bibendum's successful implantation in North America since 1975 explains the high level recognition by the American public; the company has modern industrial facilities well-adapted to the local automobile industry and a substantial resource of potential in its workforce. These are prime conditions for Bibendum to remain the technological leader in his sphere. Thirteen factories and several research and test centres ensure a strong presence in the United States.

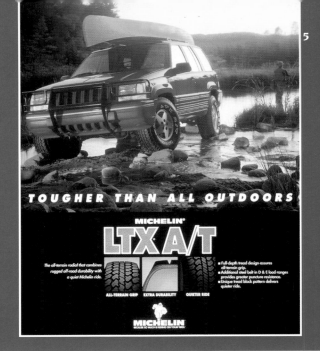

TOUGHER THAN ALL OUTDOORS

MICHELIN®

LTX A/T

The all-terrain radial that combines
rugged off-road durability with
a quiet Michelin ride.

ALL-TERRAIN GRIP   EXTRA DURABILITY   QUIETER RIDE

■ Full-depth tread design assures
all-terrain grip.
■ Additional steel belt in D & E load ranges
provides greater puncture resistance.
■ Unique tread block pattern delivers
quieter ride.

MICHELIN
BECAUSE SO MUCH IS RIDING ON YOUR TIRES

❺

United States
"Tougher than all outdoors"
"Michelin LTX A/T"
"Because so much is riding on your tires"
Language: English
Product presented: "LTX A/T"
500 x 700mm

❻

International
"We take care of the fine details
Make sure it's a Michelin"
Language: English
Corporate poster
910 x 610mm

...And this detail revealed by the
magnifying glass - it's Bibendum himself,
guarantee of quality and reliability!

We take
the fine

Details like these tell a lot about product design and precision engineering.
So it's no wonder your customers keep coming back for the Michelin quality.

United States, 1988
"Enjoy the good times with the "XCH4"
from Michelin
Because so much is riding on your tires"
Language: English
Product presented: "XCH4" tyre
950 x 1210mm

care of details.

6

fact, Michelin spends far more on Research & Development than any other
re manufacturer world-wide, making sure of future business.

MAKE SURE IT'S A MICHELIN

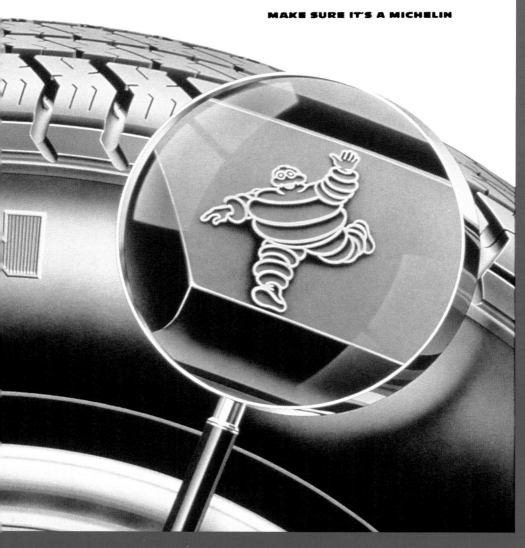

Bibendum in Canada

Michelin's four Canadian factories are
located in the province of Nova Scotia.
Canadian production is mainly intended
for original equipment on American
cars. Another part equips Japanese
and Korean cars in the North
American market.

High technology on the billboards

The 1985-1990 campaign objectives were to show the Research & Development department's capabilities, putting the accent on technology.

On TV, an "in-house" engineer writes miles of equations on a road and we see with amazement how complex a tyre is, how its shape changes when cornering, the various stresses it must handle. The posters use a variety of visuals in the same way: a digital tyre changes its shape to accommodate a stone (cf "The Michelin tyre drinks up obstacles".); or in a sharp turn, a laser image shows its precision; a computer studies water evacuation, etc. In the margin of these strong technological posters, infrequent in advertising, Bibendum speeds forward, confident of his product and its innovations.

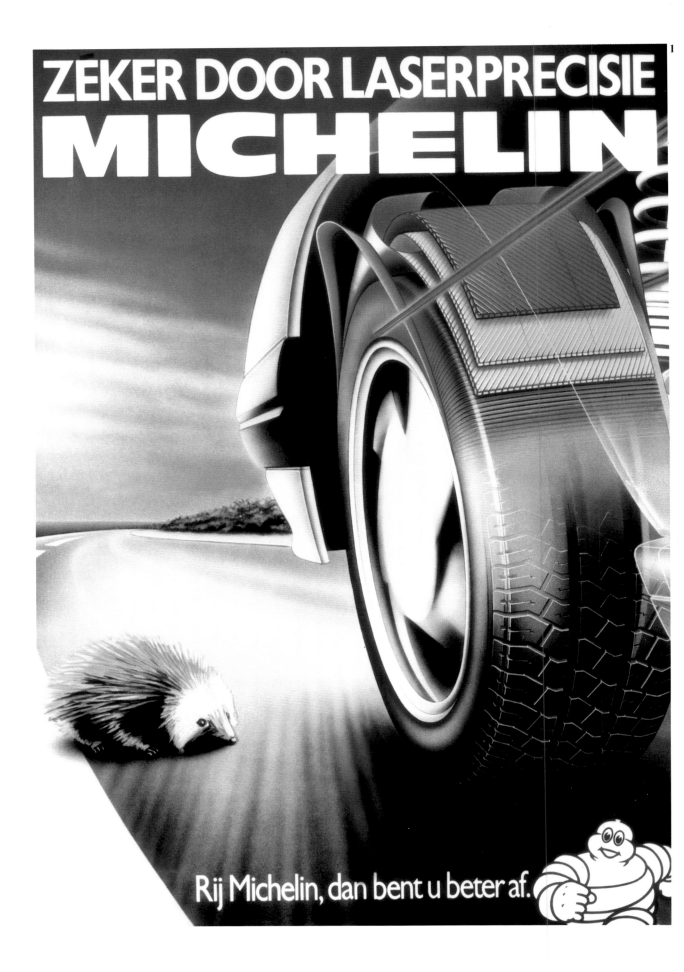

SA GOMME PEUT S'ALLONGER 5 FOIS.
LE MX ABSORBE L'IMPREVU.

MICHELIN

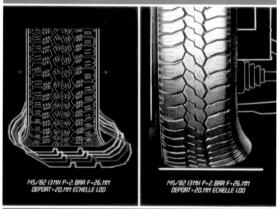

MICHELIN MX
IL RESISTE A 50000
VIRAGES A L'HEURE

145/82 13MX P•2.BAR F•26.MM
DEPORT•20.MM ECHELLE 1.00

145/82 13MX P•2.BAR F•26.MM
DEPORT•20.MM ECHELLE 1.00

MICHELIN MX
LE PNEU INFATIGABLE

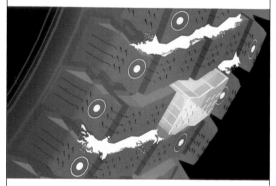

VI GIR DEG
2.000 GRUNNER TIL Å
VELGE VÅRE VINTERDEKK:
LAMELLENE.

MICHELIN
- det suverene lamelldekket

SO RUND WIE DER LASER GERADE IST.

MICHELIN

1

The Netherlands, 1989
"Laser-precision accuracy
Driving Michelin means driving
without worries"
Language: Dutch
Corporate poster
490 x 700mm

In passing (or rather in braking!) it can be
noted that a hedgehog can even be saved as
he crosses the road...a way of putting a little
life in this very technical demonstration.

2

France, 1989
"Its rubber can stretch to five times
its original size
The MX absorbs the unexpected"
Language: French
Product presented: "MX" tyre
800 x 600mm

3

France, 1987
"The Michelin "MX"
stands up to 50 000 cornerings an hour
The Michelin "MX" is the tireless tyre"
Language: French
Product presented: "MX" tyre
600 x 810mm

4

Norway, 1989
"We give you 2 000 good reasons for
choosing our winter tyres: their sipes"
Language: Norwegian
Corporate poster
500 x 700mm

5

Germany, 1989
"As round as a laser is linear
Michelin is the shortest way to safety"
Language: German
Corporate poster
600 x 840mm

Michelin in Germany

Bibendum has been commercially
present in Germany since 1906. The
present-day production from six
factories - for original equipment as
well as for the Home Trade
replacement market - is especially
appreciated by the great automobile
makers such as Mercedes, the
VAG-Audi-Seat-Skoda Group,
Ford-Germany, etc.

Bibendum, champion of endurance

The Le Mans 24-Hour Race certainly remains in the minds of fans as the height of automobile competition, together with the Indianapolis 500 in the United States, of course. To celebrate its victories on the Sarthe racing circuit, Michelin has published many promotional posters. In addition to the classic designs meant for Thailand, Japan and France, where racing cars can be seen tearing down the track, the Michelin Studio poster's graphics recall the adventures of Michel Vaillant, the great French comic book driver. Invariably present in this area of competition, Bibendum, a regular presence on the podium, does not hesitate to appear as a double of himself to congratulate himself. A simple image that brings a smile, but what power in the message!

❶

France, 1993
"At the finishing line of the Le Mans 24-Hour Race, the previous year's winner came in the most sportsmanlike way to congratulate this year's winner. Michelin First Place in the Le Mans 24-Hour Race 1992 and 1993"
Language: French
Event-related promotional poster
320 x 420mm

❷

Europe, 1988
"Super-Cup Winner"
Language: German
Event-related promotional poster
Illustration: J.B.
840 x 600mm

A l'arrivée des 24 Heures du Mans, le vainqueur de l'année dernière est venu très sportivement féliciter le vainqueur de cette année.

Michelin 1er au 24 Heures du Mans 1992 et 1993.

MICHELIN

Le Mans, samedi, 16 heures, le départ lancé. Hunaudières, les premiers rebondisse-surpuissants, le petit matin, la fatigue. droite, le drapeau à damier, la délivrance performances et de fiabilité. Un vrai fier d'inscrire à nouveau à son palmarès l'une des courses les plus prestigieuses du sport automobile, remercie et félicite Peugeot, Toyota, et tous les concurrents qui lui ont fait confiance.

400 km/h dans la ligne droite des ments, la nuit, la ronde des phares dimanche, 16 heures, la dernière ligne et le champagne à flots. 24 heures de défi pour les pneumatiques. Michelin,

N° 1 EN COMPÉTITION. N° 1 EN TECHNOLOGIE.

SUPER-CUP-SIEGER 1988
Jean-Louis Schlesser
Sauber Mercedes C 9-88

WORLD CHAMPION ③

MICHELIN
DEMAND THE BEST
MICHELIN

POUR ETRE N°1 AUX 24 H. DU MANS, IL FAUT ETRE N°1 EN TECHNOLOGIE. ④

MICHELIN

ル・マン ミシュラン2連覇。⑤

'93 61st LeMans 24 Hours

THE TIRE
MICHELIN

Bibendum goes the distance

The history of the Le Mans 24-Hour Race includes many a Bibendum victory. From the start in 1923, when a Chenard and Walker, driven by Lagache and Léonard, came in first on a 17 kilometre-long racing circuit, Michelin has been winning. The real beginnings of Bibendum in endurance runs, however, were in 1951 with a victorious Lancia on "X" tyres, then in 1965 with a Renault Alpine and a Panhard DB/CD. Michelin found victory again at Le Mans in 1978 with a Renault Alpine A 442 B. In 1989 Sauber-Mercedes and Michelin won on a 13.5 kilometre-track. This same year Schlesser, in a Mercedes, became world champion in sports car racing (WSPC). In 1992 Bibendum carried off the cup with a Peugeot 905, as in 1993. In 1995 the number one position was achieved for the first time by a one-seater vehicle, the MTR, on Michelin tyres. Bibendum was victorious with the new MacLaren F1 GTR, owing to its new rain tyres. In 1996 Bibendum won a GT1 victory again with the new Porsche, and again a GT2 victory with a Roock Racing team Porsche. In 1997 Michelin equipped almost half of all competition vehicles with 4 Prototypes, 14 GT1s and 7 GT2s and took prominent place with a McLaren GT1.

ことしも、JTCCを熱くするのは
ミシュランです。⑥

その高性能は、日本のために。
MICHELIN

Bibendum the globe-trotter

From EuroDisney Paris to Greece, and from Canada to the European Red Guide of "good restaurants", the small bookshop posters promoting Michelin publications rival each other in originality, often with Bibendum's complicity. The only exception to this "Bibendumania", the Canadian poster (2) shows a maple leaf and three Green Guides, another way of raising Michelin to the rank of being a true institution...

1 ....

Canada, 1983
"In Greece...with the new Michelin Green Guide"
Language: French
Product presented: Guides
460 x 610mm

En Grèce...
Avec le nouveau guide vert

MICHELIN

∘ Aperçus historiques
∘ Itinéraires touristiques
∘ Photographies en couleurs

Société canadienne des pneus Michelin, Ltée—Montréal, Canada   704/04-83

Troublefree travel with Bibendum

Michelin publications hold a leading position in the European travel publishing world; over 400 different products and services bring Michelin know-how to travellers in 70 countries, through some 35 000 sales outlets. Around 13 million maps, town plans and atlases, 3 million Green Guides and 1.5 million Red Guides are sold annually worldwide.
Established in Paris in 1900, Michelin's Tourism Department has been as active in North America as in Europe. The entire graphic production process - outside the photoengraving and printing - is handled in-house. Since 1989, in addition to the paper media, a new product line has used telematic and digital services to supply information, available faster, more comprehensive and more up-to-date. The itinerary calculation service on Minitel (in France), CD-ROM databases; today, all this is part of continually trying to make as much quality service available to as many customers as possible. And Michelin on the Internet must not be forgotten:
www.michelin.travel.com
which sends detailed itineraries on request for a small fee.

5

Mexico, 1988
"Banamex and Michelin...
Take Mexico in your hands"
Language: Spanish
Product presented: Green Guides
610 x 400mm

6

Spain, 1985
"Leave for your trip with the famous
Michelin Guide - Spain and
Portugal 1985"
Language: Spanish
Product presented: Red Guide
300 x 420mm

7

Italy, 1985
"Michelin Red Guide Italy, serving
motorists for 30 years"
Language: Italian
Product presented: Red Guide
360 x 170mm

8

France, 1997
"Michelin Red Guide 1997"
Language: French
Product presented: Red Guide
300 x 420mm

9

Sweden, 1991
"Aim for the stars"
Language: Swedish
Product presented: Red Guide
600 x 210mm

10

France, 1992
"3615 Michelin,
your detailed itinerary..."
Language: French
Product presented: Minitel
1000 x 1000mm

In 1989 Michelin introduced a
computerised route finding service on the
French Minitel system (3615 Michelin)
thus launching the first of a new generation
of non-paper products. The service was
extended to all Europe in 1992 and now
responds to millions of requests annually.

12

The Red Guide's eternal youth

"The original Bibendum congratulates today's Bibendum". A juxtaposition which mimics the poster for the Le Mans 24-Hour Race (page 30). To celebrate the first 100 years of Michelin as a company, founded in 1889 in Clermont-Ferrand, the Red Guide France gave its readers a first edition facsimile of the now unobtainable 1900 Red Guide.

....11

France, 1989
"Michelin gives you a reprint
of the 1900 Guide".
Language: French
Event-related promotional poster
300 x 460mm

....12

Great Britain, 1989
"Special offer"
Language: English
Event-related promotional poster
300 x 420mm

A surprising premonition

"This publication was born with the century and will last just as long. Motoring has just been born and it will develop each year and the tyre with it, because the tyre is the essential part without which an automobile cannot move..."
This premonitory preface shows how clear and far-reaching the Michelin brothers' vision in 1900 was of the automobile's future and its roles. After having contributed greatly to the development of the hotel and restaurant industry, thereby also becoming a useful tool for general tourism and the renown of the French welcome, the Michelin Red Guide, soon to be a hundred years old, still has a long life ahead.

Airbrushing and hyperrealism for the MX

All those interested by modern art will appreciate the work of the Hyperrealists; some of their paintings look, at first glance, like photographs. These works are often signed by "airbrush magicians". This little painting pistol makes it possible to produce many light effects, owing to the many possibilities in the play of superposition. Since the early 1960s advertising has been regularly interested in this technique, which, owing to its precision and its "readability", has been well received by the public. The luminous quality and the optical effects of these posters opposite are quite characteristic. For example, the old city brightly lit by the light of Italy's moon, puts the MXV tyre in the limelight; but so does the poster from the Michelin Paris Studio - a tilted wheel shows much of the tyre, with the wet motorway stretching out before it. The effect of realism is arresting. Bibendum himself benefits from this technique on two British posters, where he is put into particularly becoming - and unaccustomed - relief. Note the strong reddish-orange tones, similar to those of the Turkish poster showing the three Bibendums on a beach with a setting sun.

EVEN BETTER VALUE.

MICHELIN MX

Yeni MXT
DAHA GÜÇLÜ KAVRAMA,
DAHA UZUN ÖMÜR...

65 80 70

MICHELIN ///// MXT

KALİTESİ, GÜVENLİĞİ VE RAHATLIĞI KIYASLANAMAZ.

MICHELIN MX

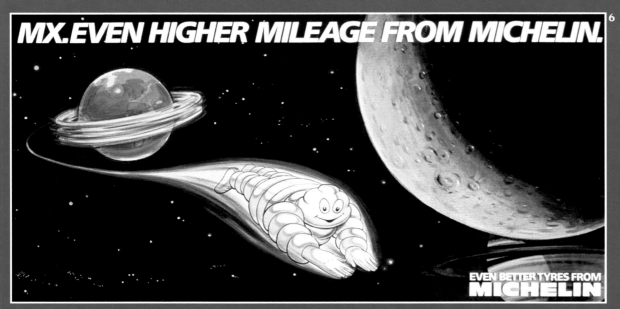

MX. EVEN HIGHER MILEAGE FROM MICHELIN.

EVEN BETTER TYRES FROM
MICHELIN

This English poster evokes the distance
from the Earth to the Moon, in order to
give the MX tyre credit for a high mileage.
Here we find once more the theme of
Bibendum in space.

Bibendum in Italy

Bibendum has sold his tyres in Italy
since 1901 from the Michelin sales
headquarters in Milan. Five years later
the company chose Turin, Italian capital
of the automobile, to build its first
factory outside France. The Michelin
brothers' idea, which they then
delegated to Adolphe Daubrée, was to
have a production site near their
principal customers, such as the
Fabbrica Italiana Automobili di Torino,
better known as Fiat.

Bibendum, Prince of the Desert

In Arab countries, and especially in the desert regions, driving conditions are particularly arduous. If the animals are adapted for survival in extreme temperatures, it must be the same for the vehicles and even more so for their tyres. This eye-catching poster, baptised the "Desert Animals", summarises succinctly this message and is an excellent introduction to the Paris-Dakar Rally posters; during the last ten years Michelin has won all car, motorcycle and truck categories of the race.

I ....

International, 1990
"Which of them can resist temperatures of 80° for a long time? Michelin MXTE - Safe and resistant at all temperatures"
Language: English
Product presented: MXTE tyre

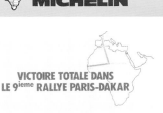

VICTOIRE TOTALE DANS
LE 9ieme RALLYE PARIS-DAKAR

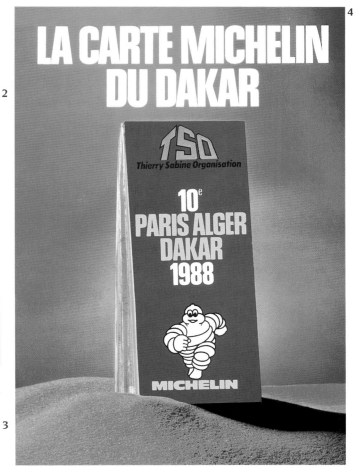

LA CARTE MICHELIN
DU DAKAR

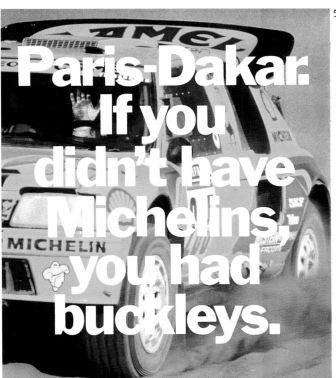

The first two cars across the line in this year's gruelling Paris-Dakar Rally used Michelin tyres exclusively. As did the first nine motorbikes and the first truck. What further proof do you need of Michelin's reliability under the toughest driving conditions? Demand the best.
MICHELIN

Bibendum in Saudi Arabia

A country of great contrasts, where luxuriant vegetation and modern cities juxtapose sandy and arid conditions. Saudi Arabia represents a very large tyre market. Established here since the 1960s, Bibendum has adapted to the specific environment of this country and is now well known for the quality of his products. Today Saudi Arabia has a road network of 33 000 kilometres of surfaced roads (as opposed to only 3 000 km twenty years ago). There are about 2 million cars and as many vans or trucks. Top-of-the-range tyres occupy a large share of the Saudi Arabian market.

Bibendum's great comeback

1986, Billboards in France are covered with posters showing close-ups of the face, or a hand, or even a foot; pieces of Bibendum presented against a background of brilliant colours: orange, mint green, purple, egg-yolk yellow, etc. This cutting up of the "Michelin Man" was particularly audacious; as if challenging the public's immediate recognition.
The basic idea of this campaign was to recall the Michelin "fundamentals":
- "Three hundred ways of saying Tyre", for the international dimension,
- "Two billion wheels won over", for the market share,
- "Sold in three thousand sizes", for the variety of the products on offer,
- "The year 2000 is already here", for the high technology, etc.
The results were as positive as hoped, this campaign being saluted by advertising professionals as being one of the best over the preceding ten years. For the young advertising firm, BDDP, to whom Michelin had just entrusted its account, this was a historic event. Since then, the agency has continued to develop and promote Michelin communications in Europe, in Africa, in the Middle East and in parts of Asia.

5

France, 1988
"Everyone on Michelin!"
Language: French
Corporate poster
400 x 280mm

France, 1986
"The year 2000 is already here"
Language: French
Corporate poster
400 x 280mm

Tout le monde en Michelin!

5

6

L'an 2000 déjà atteint.

7
France, 1988
"What is there to do? What to see?
Ask him"
Language: French
Product presented: Maps and Green Guides
590 x 420mm

8
France, 1988
"What is there to do? What to see?"
Language: French
Product presented: Maps and Green Guides
590 x 420mm

The BDDP 1988 campaign for Maps and
Guides took up other "fundamentals":
like a Woody Hallen interrogation, the
agency repositioned Maps and Green
Guides on their original mission:
to inform their readers who ask,
"What is there to do? What to see?"

BDDP, good at "disruption"

It only took the French team BDDP
(standing for Jean-Claude Boulet,
Jean-Marie Dru, Marie-Catherine Dupuy,
Jean-Pierre Petit) a few years to go from
the embryonic stage to the level of
being an international agency for
marketing and communications.
Founded in 1984 by these experienced
publicity professionals, this agency
"unlike the others" had all it took to
convince Michelin to entrust BDDP with
its communications. This was due
primarily to the theory of "disruption",
fine-tuned by Jean-Marie Dru. With this
method communication campaigns are
devised to break with the practices of
competitors, while staying closer to
public perception of Michelin's image:
a commercial enterprise capable of
communicating with honesty, always
close to the customer. Yet Michelin had
also been able to take risks in its
history, to rely on intuition and refuse
convention. Once this analysis had been
completed BDDP could start to create
its strategy by selecting the intangible
core values and other values with a
potential for evolution.

"My name is Bib... Bibendum"

All those who remember Her Majesty's Secret Service agent's famous line will smile at this title. Nevertheless, Bibendum did indeed save Ian Fleming's hero - in a film. In fact, the secret agent finds himself locked in the boot of a Rolls Royce which has been pushed into a lake, and he survives the prolonged immersion owing to the air contained in one of the tyres! As can be seen on these posters, James Bond and Bibendum are a team and are perfectly complementary. It should be noted that there are several variations on this theme. The one showing an armed James Bond (1) was judged as too violent, and instead the project with the simply drawn tyre was preferred. These posters are the work of Walter Storozuk, an American illustrator, who orchestrated Bibendum's return to the limelight, in particular, by drawing the famous "Running Bibendum" from the 1980s.

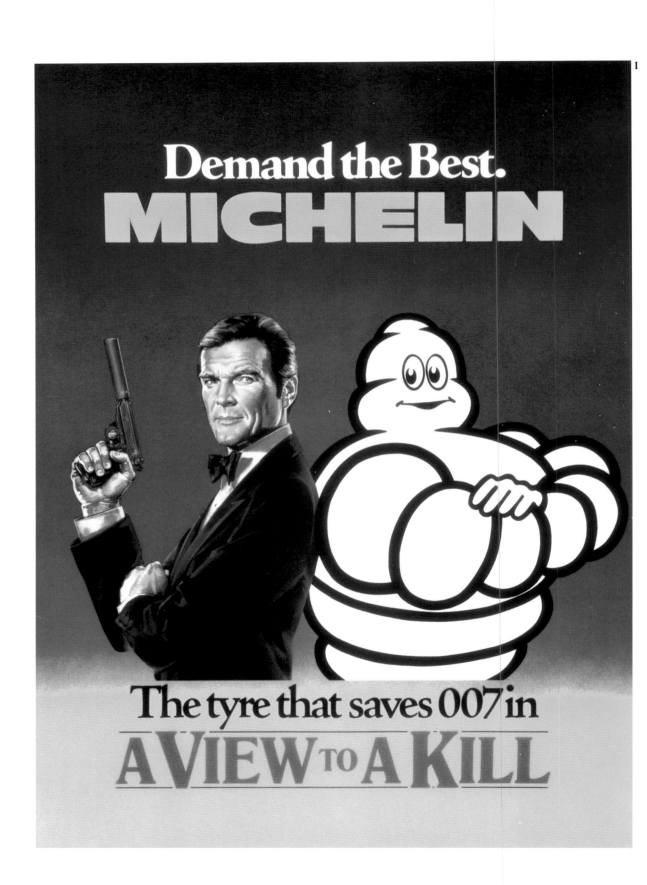

1

Great Britain, 1986
"Demand the Best. Michelin, the tyre that saves 007 in "A View to A Kill"
Language: English
Event-related promotional poster
500 x 680mm

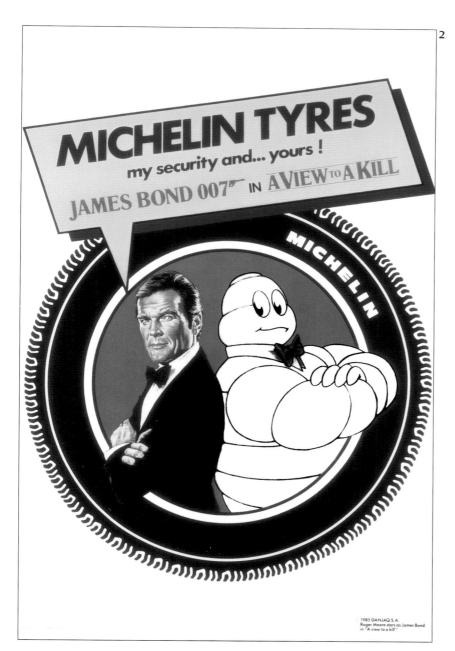

2

Great Britain, 1985
"Michelin tyres, my security and...yours!"
Language: English
Event-related promotional poster
420 x 615mm

3

Great Britain, 1985
"See how Michelin saves James Bond 007
in "A View to A Kill"
Language: English
Event-related promotional poster
420 x 615mm

These two posters made their way around
the globe, the two heroes framed by a tyre,
back to back in perfect symmetry right
down to the black bow-tie!

When the snow tyre shows its difference

Each winter for some years now Bibendum has delighted us with his snow tyre campaign. Among the best of recent posters, the Norwegian bear and his "tread" is a perfect illustration of the superiority of simplicity in graphic advertising; another is the ice-sculpted tyre in Germany; or the "molto simpatico" Bibendum driving a tyre, leaving a trail of springtime behind him. Winter conditions make it necessary for Bibendum to press forward in the snow only if he is wrapped in warm clothes, with a woolly scarf and cap...even in the Alpin Y "snow scene"! A beautiful example of adaptation to the natural surroundings.

❶...
France, 1997
Photo of the poster "Alpin tyre with Y tread" on advertising billboard

❷...
*Norway, 1987
"The new benchmark tyre for snow and ice! Michelin 200 - take it to the limit with the new tyre for Norway"*
Language: Norwegian
Product presented: XM + S tyre
560 x 800mm

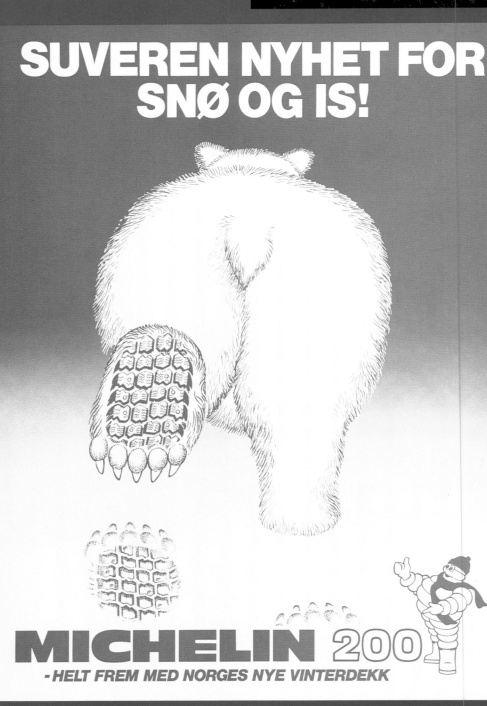

Bibendum in Scandinavia

Michelin has been present commercially
in Scandinavia since the late 1920s
(Sweden, 1927; Denmark, 1927;
Norway, 1931; Finland, 1932); that is, at
the time when the first snow tyre was
designed and commercialised.

Bibendum on the attack for an international image

To see Bibendum on top of a podium explaining that "the amazing thing about Michelin tyres is not that they cost a little more... it's how little more they cost" could be a bit surprising. Nevertheless, this is the point of this poster in English from the mid-1980s. A comparative tyre image study conducted in North America shows that Michelin is the leader by a wide margin according to the following criteria: "exceptional quality"; brand with benchmark status; "technological advance; name prestige".

Between 1980 and 1991, several corporate campaigns were launched. Bibendum was not omnipresent, but he was far from having disappeared (see 2 and 4). As for the poster with the "Hi-Fi" tyres, it is said that the Michelin Paris Studio illustrators long wondered if they should use a gramophone record or a CD, a device that was little known at the time. It was finally decided that the more recognisable of the two - the gramophone record - would increase the impact of the message.

The amazing thing about Michelin tyres is not that they cost a little more...it's how little more they cost.

Demand the best.
MICHELIN

2

Une griffe rassurante

MICHELIN

Michelin

La qualité qui dure.

3

MICHELIN
Les pneus haute fidélité

4

ROULEZ MICHELIN
pour tirer le maximum
de votre voiture

MICHELIN
ça rassure!

5

MICHELIN
A COMPLETE RANGE
OF HIGH MILEAGE
RADIALS

ميشلان
MICHELIN

Keeping Nigeria moving

Factory
MICHELIN TYRES
MADE IN NIGERIA

6

7

MICHELIN

Bibendum in Nigeria

Michelin runs several rubber plantations in Africa's most populated country. The hot and humid climate, as well as the nature of the soil, are perfect for developing this type of activity. A tyre production unit was established in the capital Port-Harcourt in 1962 and it produces essentially for the local market. Michelin also has commercial bases in the Ivory Coast (since 1954), Senegal (since 1955), the Cameroons and Mali (since 1958).

49

"Left 90°, 3rd,
5 000 revs; 100 metres,
right 30°, 4th,
step on it..."

Bibendum goes full speed ahead in rallies

This poster bears witness to the imagination and know-how of the Michelin Paris Studio and takes advantage of photographic methods with a very dynamic shot of Timo Salonen's Peugeot 205; then three small photos at an angle, like a contact print. But this photo's surprise, which gives it its power, is Bibendum, a sort of desert giant, who accompanies the team and gives the car the necessary endurance.
It should be noted that the "Running Bib" drawing is a signature particularly well adapted to the sports competition posters, especially when they end, as they invariably do, in victories!

❶

France, 1985
"Michelin,
1985 world rally champion
Michelin - Progress on the move"
Language: French
590 x 420mm

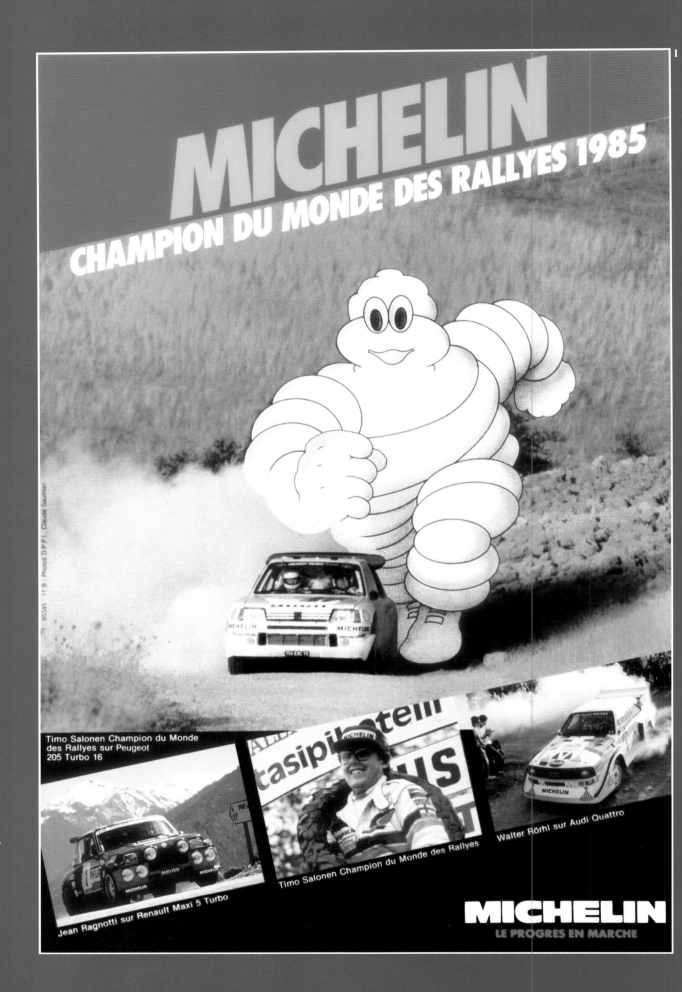

2

France, 1982
"Fiftieth Monte Carlo Rally
Fourth victory in five years!
Michelin X Radial tyre"
Language: French
610 x 450mm

3

France, 1988
"For Michelin
each victory is a new departure
1988 Monte Carlo Rally"
Language: French
610 x 800mm

4

Sweden, 1986
"The tyres that win. Sweden Rally"
Language: Swedish
700 x 500mm

5

Japan, 1992
"Paris-Moscow-Peking Marathon Raid"
Language: Japanese and English
700 x 500mm

Bibendum on small roads and tracks

Michelin introduced the radial tyre in rallies in 1965. In 1973, Bibendum carried off the first world rally championship with the radial on the Renault Alpine. Between 1982 and 1996, Bibendum won the world champion title 11 times with the following rally drivers and cars: Rohrl with Opel, Mäkinen with Mitsubishi, Mikkola and Blomqvist with Audi, Salonen with Peugeot, Kankkunen with Peugeot, Lancia and Toyota, Biasion with Lancia and Auriol with Toyota.

1977
1985

The United States welcome the radial

Humour is often present in Bibendum's communications. As an example, the poster shows him standing on a small podium decorated with the American colours. Wearing an Uncle Sam hat, a tyre over his shoulder, he is haranguing a crowd of demonstrators brandishing placards in favour of the radial tyre. This allusion to political support groups and the protest marches in front of the White House is especially appreciated at a time (the 1970s) when consumer associations in the United States are beginning to call for higher quality tyres.

I ....

*United States, 1977
"Join the Michelin Movement
X steel-belted radials for American passenger cars!
ZX steel-belted radials for imported cars!
XAS steel-belted radials for imported sports cars!"
Language: English
Product presented: X, ZX, XAS
car tyres
810 x 610mm*

THAT'S HOW MANY MILES THE NEW MICHELIN XA4 RADIAL WAS TESTED.

As far as we know, no other tire company goes to these lengths to test a new radial.

But then again, no other tire company has the Michelin name to live up to. So if it takes 20 million miles before we'll put a new radial on the market, so be it.

That's why we built the largest tire testing ground in America. Then filled it with equipment that lets us mercilessly test

things like lateral adhesion and controllability. How the tire performs in water and snow or on ice. How long it lasts. And dozens of other attributes we need to know.

But we don't limit our tests to our testing grounds. Each new radial model is given to professional drivers all over the country. All they do is drive. And drive. And drive.

After millions of miles of testing, we then give each new

model to companies that run fleets of vehicles like taxis and limousines. So millions more miles are put on the tires.

Still we're not satisfied. So we invented testing equipment that coarsely simulates road conditions. And we put even more millions of miles on our tires.

The new Michelin XA4 all season radial was tested this way. And after 20,000,000 miles, we knew we had a tire

that performed like a snow tire in snow. A highway tire on dry pavement. And a tire designed for the rain when the going got wet. And that, with proper care, it could keep on performing for up to sixty thousand miles.

After all, when a tire is tested that twenty million miles, wouldn't you expect anything less?

MICHELIN. BECAUSE SO MUCH IS RIDING ON YOUR TIRES.

2

2 - United States, 1985
"Michelin: Celebrating Ten Years of
Manufacturing in the U.S.A"
Language: English
710 x 485mm

Event-related promotional poster, for the
tenth anniversary of the Greenville factory
in South Carolina

3

United States, 1985
"20 million. That's how many miles
the new Michelin XA4 radial was tested
Michelin. Because so much
is riding on your tyres"
Language: English
Product presented: XA4 tyre
320 x 470mm

Note that Bibendum is standing like
Hercules, legs and arms wide apart,
carrying a "beautiful American"...

4

United States, 1983
Go for it with Michelin!
Michelin. We put America on radials
Language: English
In-house poster

Bibendum triumphs with the radial

American cars, heavy and powerful; an extensive motorway network; and local customs and driving rules led the Michelin USA researchers to conceive tyres specifically adapted to the North American market. In 1980 radial tyres represent about 60% of all tyres on the market (original equipment and replacement), the figure was only 15% at the beginning of the 1970s. These figures alone describe how far the radial had come...its superiority was therefore sufficient in itself so that all manufacturers were led to adopt it. Michelin has retained an image of innovation and high quality, which have been very valuable in establishing itself in the American market. The quality of manufacturing and the performance on the road are recognised by both end-users and car manufacturers.

Bibendum at the wheel in Europe

As this poster implies, the general public is unaware that Michelin is an important wheel producer. The company supplies tyre and wheel assemblies to motor vehicle manufacturers.

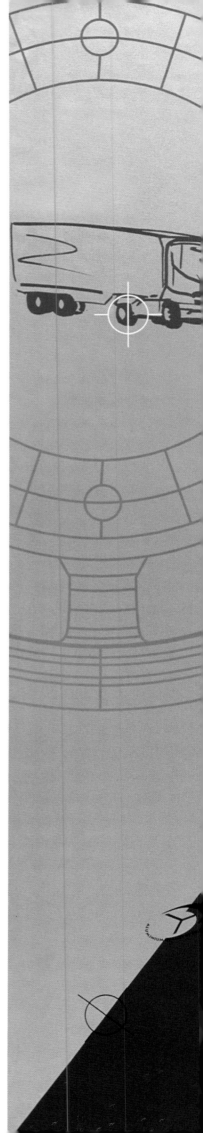

DID YOU KNOW THAT MICHELIN ALSO MAKE WHEELS ?

MICHELIN® INOVIAL

International
"Did you know that Michelin also
make wheels?
Michelin Inovial".
Language: English
Corporate poster
Creation: Michelin Paris Studio
600 x 800mm

Bibendum, "heavyweight" champion

Bibendum, who loves getting around in a truck or a van, has a great friendship with the professionals of the road. The long-distance truck drivers are among his most fervent admirers and, for certain of them, this can even be considered a passion as witnessed by the many "truck Bibs" which not only adorn trucks throughout Europe, but also in North America, in Africa and Asia.

I ....

Thailand, 1993
"Three types of tyres for three functions Michelin, there is nothing better for your pick-up"
Language: Thai and English
Product presented: XCE2, XCE, XCP2
560 x 800mm

This is a thermoformed poster, making Bibendum appear slightly in relief

2

Greece
"Michelin XCA, a robust companion
for your van"
Language: Greek
Product presented: XCA tyre

3

Egypt, 1990
"Michelin XCE
New radial tyre for vans"
Language: Arabic
Product presented: XCE tyre
600 x 800mm

4

Austria, 1982
"The truck drivers get on the road
and transport for you".
Language: German
Corporate poster
600 x 800mm

Bibendum in Brazil

"Michelin Brazil", a dream which came
true in 1981 with the construction in the
State of Rio of two production units.
Up to then, there had been no other
Michelin industrial plant in Latin
America. Brazil was chosen, because in
this immense country, 90% of goods are
transported by road. The many road
hauliers were eager to welcome the
radial. Two local rubber plantations
provide the natural rubber for the
Brazilian production.

International
"Michelin XZY radial"
Product presented: XZY tyre
600 x 800mm

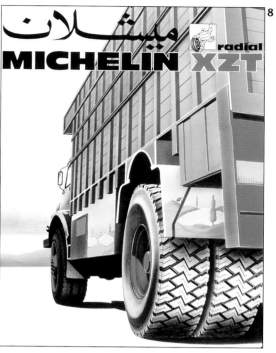

Stick your load to the road.

A heavier responsibility rests on the drive axle than any other, so Michelin have designed a tyre specially to cope. No amount of torque will put the XZT in a spin. Optimum power is put down evenly on the road. Slush and water are, literally, shrugged off by integral 'clearing' channels to give excellent grip in all conditions. And take a load off your mind.

Switch to **MICHELIN**
More running, less running costs.

Tough as old boots.

The Michelin XZY is tough enough to soak up punishment off the road, whether working in a quarry, in a building site or on an unmetalled road. And yet it has a very cool on-the-road performance. And, just like your old boots, the XZY will give you a long trouble free tread life. It can also be regrooved, remoulded and finally regrooved again. In fact, you could call it the sole of reliability.

Switch to **MICHELIN**
More running, less running costs.

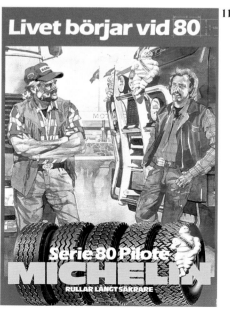

Livet börjar vid 80

Serie 80 Pilote
MICHELIN
RULLAR LÅNGT SÄKRARE

Bibendum takes to the air

Michelin *has equipped the American space shuttle since 1995. The high level of quality, conceived for especially extreme conditions, underlies the many other Bibendum achievements in the world of aviation. In the mid-1980s, the American firm McDonnell Douglas presents the F-15 E, its new combat plane conceived for the US Air Force; it is equipped with Michelin tyres. Other Michelin tyres are used today on various American or European aircraft, military or civil: the Mirage 3, F1, 2000, the Airbus A 300, A 320, the Falcon 900, etc. The world giant Boeing has also chosen to equip its great carrier, the 777, with Michelin tyres. On this poster, which is an extract of a corporate campaign showing all Michelin's products, one can see a large carrier plane at the very moment of takeoff.*

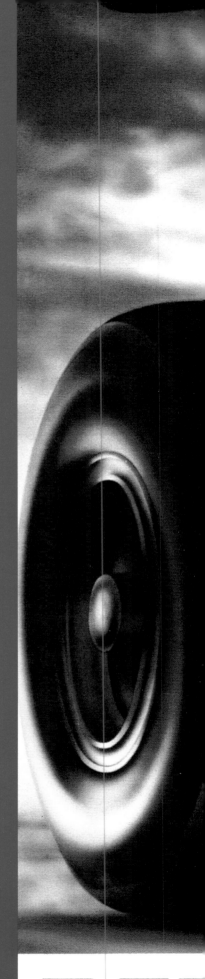

RIJ MICH

The Netherlands, 1989
"With Michelin, drive without cares"
Language: Dutch
Corporate poster
600 x 800mm

How tyres work on an Airbus A-300

At takeoff, an Airbus weighs up to 165 tonnes. Each of the ten main tyres supports close to 20 tonnes, or four times as much as a heavy vehicle of equivalent dimensions. When the pilot releases all the power of the two jet engines (24 000kg of thrust each) the plane accelerates for 50 seconds (the main tyres then turn at 1 600 revolutions per minute) the nose lifts up, which adds an additional weight of 50% or thereabouts, followed very rapidly by takeoff.

On landing, at the moment of contact with the ground, the plane is moving at about 240 kilometres an hour and the tyres go instantly from zero to 1 100 revolutions a minute. Next, the plane travels along the runway for about 1 700 metres, with intense braking created by reversing the jet's engine thrust, creating an additional weight of 70 to 100% on the forward half of the craft.

Three Michelin factories manufacture "airplane" tyres in the world: Bourges (France), Cuneo (Italy) and Norwood (USA).

CHELIN
IN, U BENT *lang* BETER AF

Bibendum in some surprising vehicles

1980 *heralded the launch of a particularly audacious poster campaign in Great Britain. Bibendum is driving vehicles which are each more surprising than the others. Fruit of the imagination of the Connell, May and Stevenson agency, this campaign shows Bibendum riding a green bean, a goldfish, a corn cob and a cottage, but he is also at the "wheel" of a great shoe, a tube of glue (see page 59) or a garden spade (see page 65). All these objects and accessories being fitted, obviously, with Michelin tyres... This campaign put Bibendum in the limelight in Great Britain and echoed the drawings of the 1920s to 1960s, where the "Michelin Man" appeared in all possible and imaginable situations; from being the motorist's friend and advisor to being that of the tourist's vade-mecum through the various Michelin Guides.*

Drive the long runner.

Switch to **MICHELIN** and insist on no other.

Sweet cornering.

Switch to **MICHELIN** and insist on no other.

Feel at home on the road.

Switch to **MICHELIN**
and insist on no other.

Get a grip in the wet.

Switch to **MICHELIN**
and insist on no other.

1

Great Britain, 1980
"Drive the long runner
Switch to Michelin and insist
on no other"
Language: English
Corporate poster
770 x 380mm

2

Great Britain, 1980
"Sweet cornering
Switch to Michelin and insist
on no other"
Language: English
Corporate poster
770 x 380mm

3

Great Britain, 1980
"Feel at home on the road
Switch to Michelin and insist
on no other"
Language: English
Corporate poster
770 x 380mm

4

Great Britain, 1980
"Get a grip in the wet
Switch to Michelin and insist
on no other"
Language: English
Corporate poster
770 x 380mm

**Bibendum and
the United Kingdom**

Since 1973 Michelin has only
made radial tyres in the United
Kingdom. The factory at
Stoke-on-Trent is devoted to the
production of tyres for cars and
vans, as well as the production of
tyre components such as steel
cord. Today, Michelin Tyre Public
Limited Company, Michelin's
subsidiary in the United Kingdom,
also produces radial pneumatic
tyres in three other factories:
Ballymena, Burnley and Dundee.

Bibendum moves mountains

Great construction sites have always been places of exception. And also, in the image of the mythological hero, Hercules, Bibendum is not afraid of massive construction projects. On the contrary, the more gigantic the project, in short, Pharaonic... the happier he is. He can then invent the outsize tyres required by such construction sites.
For example, in 1996, Michelin Spain produced the largest tyre in the world, the X Mine D2; a giant 3.72 metres in diameter, weighing 5.7 tonnes and containing close to 2 000 kilometres of steel wire reinforcement! These two posters illustrate one aspect of civil engineering, the work on the construction sites. One is practically corporate, the other belonged to the "Switch to Michelin" campaign (see also page 62), presenting a Bibendum who is obviously delighted to be playing with a garden spade...

❶
The Netherlands, 1990
"With Michelin, drive without cares"
Language: Dutch
Corporate poster
600 x 800mm

MICHELIN
RIJ MICHELIN, U BENT *lang* BETER AF

Save a pile on fuel.

Michelin earthmover radial tyres, well known for their aggressive traction, and long working life, can also slash your fuel bills.

They have a lower rolling resistance than energy-absorbing crossplies. So much lower, in fact, that in RAC-monitored tests, average fuel savings of 9.38% were recorded over terrain that makes muck shifting such 'thirsty' work. Add that up over a working year and the savings will amount to a tidy pile.

For details contact: Michelin Earthmover Division, 81 Fulham Road, London SW3 6RD. Telephone 01-589 1460 or ring your nearest Michelin Branch.

Switch to **MICHELIN**

Great Britain, 1982
"Save a pile on fuel.
Switch to Michelin"
Language: English
Corporate poster

The twelve labours of Bibendum

To be present everywhere in the field of civil engineering, Michelin has fine-tuned various ranges of tyre products for construction site machinery (loaders, bulldozers, levellers...). As for transport equipment (dumpers, diggers...) it is the same objective: tyres for ground going from soft and malleable to rocky, hard and abrasive tracks while going at a reasonable speed, without forgetting special tyres for desert-like conditions on inconsistent ground and tracks. Finally, Bibendum, who most decidedly thinks of everything, even offers tyres for underground mines. As for the technicians and engineers, they travel throughout the world to visit construction sites and to study on-the-spot any particular problems that are raised.

Four Michelin factories throughout the world manufacture earthmover tyres: Le Puy-en-Velay (France - 1977), Montceau-les-Mines (France - 1971), Vitoria (Spain - 1966) and Lexington (USA).

Bibendum crops up in the fields!

Magnificent! There is no other word to describe this poster which will certainly remain in the annals of advertising as a masterpiece of simplicity. Created for the Salon d'Agriculture in Paris in 1996 and for a 4 x 3 metre billboard campaign throughout Europe, it is one of the best examples of putting Bibendum in the limelight. But BDDP's marvellous idea was not so easy to realise. It required all the experience and professionalism of their Swiss subsidiary Boch & Butz to achieve the final result.

1

Europe, 1996
Corporate poster
Photomontage
4000 x 3000mm

2

France, 1979
"Michelin Bib'X radial"
Language: French
Product presented: BIB'X
840 x 630mm

3

Great Britain, 1982
"Crops up all over the country
Switch to Michelin".
Language: English
Corporate poster: agricultural tyre

Crops up all over the country.

The same qualities that have made Michelin radials number one with operators on the road, are making farmers switch in their field.
Longer life, keener handling, better grip and flotation, lower rolling resistance – they're at the root of Michelin's comprehensive range of agricultural tyres.
Helping to push costs down – and crops up.

Switch to **MICHELIN**

66

4

France, 1994
"The new Michelin 4 x 4. City gear you
can wear in the country"
Language: French, also in Dutch (extract)

Picking up on the idea of Bibendum's foot
(page 41, no 4), this 4 x 4 campaign goes
even further to present the new all-terrain
vehicle tyre. Becoming half farmer, half city
dweller, here Bibendum, exceptionally,
has lost his usual boots.

5

The Netherlands, 1990
"Ask for the information sheet on Michelin's
agricultural tyre sponsoring"
Language: Dutch
Product presented: agricultural tyre
500 x 750mm

6

France, 1990
"Michelin radial technology"
Language: French
Corporate poster: Agricultural radial
240 x 550mm

Bibendum, partner in the agricultural world

Born in a region of rural tradition, Bibendum is very much attached to offering tyres for all field machinery. For tractors, according to the need, the tread and casing evolve to combine adhesion, damage resistance and flexibility. There is also a range of narrow products which are suitable for row work, such as spraying and harvesting. In the forest, Michelin tyres are also at ease, whether it is a question of equipping light or heavy vehicles for difficult jobs. Michelin also supplies specific tyres for agricultural machinery operating on loose or swampy ground (rice or corn harvesting). In the sphere of agricultural trailers, tyres with circumferential tread grooves, prevent sideways movement. Bibendum also makes tyres for garden machinery and for haymaking. Two Michelin factories make agricultural tyres: Valladolid (Spain) and les Carmes (Clermont-Ferrand).

Bibendum cultivates his "greens"

Since their creation in 1926, the Green Guides have experienced growing success. They are appreciated by the true traveller who has time to plan his or her itinerary, the curiosity to learn about things and to go beyond the limits of a superficial stay. Easy to read, they make pleasant travel companions.

This poster plays on the longish format of the Green Guide making it the same height as the New York skyscrapers.

1 ....
United States, 1986
"Where to find the best view of New York
Get the Michelin Green Guide and you'll
know more about New York than
most New Yorkers"
Language: English
510 x 760mm

WHERE TO FIND THE BEST VIEW OF NEW YORK.

GET THE MICHELIN GREEN GUIDE. AND YOU'LL KNOW MORE ABOUT NEW YORK THAN MOST NEW YORKERS.

The Green Guide, a landmark in its own right

For over fifty years, Bibendum has published his Guides with the green cover, a complement to his Red Guides. Created by Michelin staff writers after having visited the sites themselves, each Green Guide speaks only of what each person has individually experienced. The Guide therefore responds to the true needs of the traveller, who, without doubt, can trust its stars and its indications about the conditions for access or visiting, the schedules, pricing, etc. The only necessary precaution for the reader: to have the latest edition. They are, indeed, brought up-to-date every 12 to 18 months... Today, taking all translations into account, the Green Guide collection has more than 170 titles, covering France, Europe and North America. It is also starting to appear in Africa and Asia.

The bicycle comes back in force

Here are three productions of the Michelin Paris Studio. First an illustration treated in a cartoon fashion for the VTT tyre. Bibendum is taking great and visible pleasure in jumping with his "Bibcross" tyres, but he is virtually absent from the two others. In a more classic style, the poster promoting the touring bicycle tyre makes us feel like going for a ride; while the third poster is very much characteristic of the 1980s, representing the bicycle being ridden on the globe. It is a balanced photomontage, in restful blue and yellowish-orange tones, with the product in the limelight and the discreet charm and tranquility of riding on Michelin.

1 ....
France, 1984
"In cyclo-crossing, Michelin is great!"
Language: French
Creation: Michelin Paris Studio
360 x 500mm

1

Bibcross 2. Des pneus modernes qui bénéficient de toute l'expérience acquise par Michelin en pneus pour moto tout-terrain : une sculpture agressive et très enveloppante pour une excellente motricité sous tous les angles ; une carcasse légère et souple qui conserve cependant un haut niveau de résistance.

5 couleurs sont proposées.

Bibcross 2 TS Compétition
Un pneu racing à tringles souples, très léger. Une sculpture tracée par ordinateur, qui allie motricité et capacité de reprise à un rendement optimum en ligne droite.

ARRIVÉE

En bicrossing MICHELIN ça arrache!

70

MICHELIN ELAN

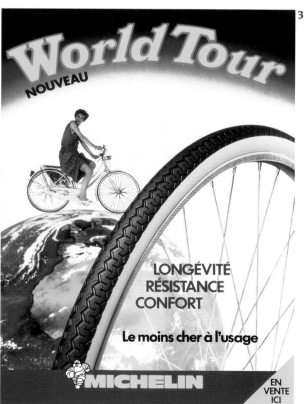

World Tour
NOUVEAU

LONGÉVITÉ
RÉSISTANCE
CONFORT

Le moins cher à l'usage

MICHELIN

EN VENTE ICI

The bicycle, forever young

In the early 1980s, bicycle tyres come back in force. Racing cyclists start to use the famous "Bib TS" (flexible tyres folded in a box) and then the "Hi-Lite" tyres. Faithful to its competition traditions, Michelin also explores new technologies in the area of bicycle tyres, making more and more modern products and services available to its customers. The KM 107 prototypes were used by three leading cycling teams in 1997. Optimising cost effectiveness, road grip, flexibility, comfort and resistance, they made it possible for Frédéric Guesdon to win the Paris-Roubaix, the greatest race classic and above all the most demanding one for tyres. From the very start of cyclo-cross racing, Bibendum saw his tyre triumph in the 1997 French championship with Mengin and at the world championship with Pontoni (Italian).

The ZX, the third-generation radial

The Michelin Paris Studio organises several outdoor poster campaigns around the new ZX tyre. These actions bear witness to a great coherency in advertising and a resolutely European vision. One will notice how often Bibendum is present, in particular with a little graphic flash of genius, that of making him "drive" a tyre; the pun about "treads" is present as well. The poster "Start out on the right tyre" plays graphically with the idea of being prepared for good and bad weather.

①
Great Britain, 1974
"Drive a Michelin.
It makes a good car better"
Language: English

Drive a Michelin.
It makes a good car better.

MICHELIN ZX RADIALS

2

France, 1974
"Surer, longer
Michelin ZX all-weather radial"
Language: French
640 x 340mm

3

France, 1975
"Back-of-the-bus" campaign, Paris

4

France, 1980
"Michelin ZX all-weather radial
Start out on the right tyre"
Language: French
Creation: Michelin Paris Studio

5

France, 1980
"In all weathers start out
on the right tyre
Michelin XZX"
Language: French
Creation: Michelin Paris Studio
640 x 840mm

The ZX under the magnifying glass

In April 1967 the first ZX tyre comes out. In October of this same year, the company begins to commercialise a "tubeless" ZX. The ZX distinguishes itself from its predecessors by its rounded shoulders, a greater number of transversal sipes and more water evacuation grooves.

Sports cars
in America

The American passion for fast
and powerful sports cars has
long been a market feature of
the States. This great love is
most notable for European cars,
especially the beautiful
Italians, British or Germans.
These imported cars are
considered the height of
prestige. Nevertheless, domestic
sports cars are gaining more
and more in strength and the
market for Mustangs, Camaros
and other Corvettes develops
increasingly.
In the 1970s Michelin is the
only manufacturer to supply
radial tyres adapted to sports
vehicles. The company is
already well known and has an
excellent image, but Bibendum,
less well known on the other
side of the ocean, has only a
symbolic presence.

United States, about 1975
"Made for each other!
Your imported car and Michelin ZX"
Language: English
Product presented: ZX tyre

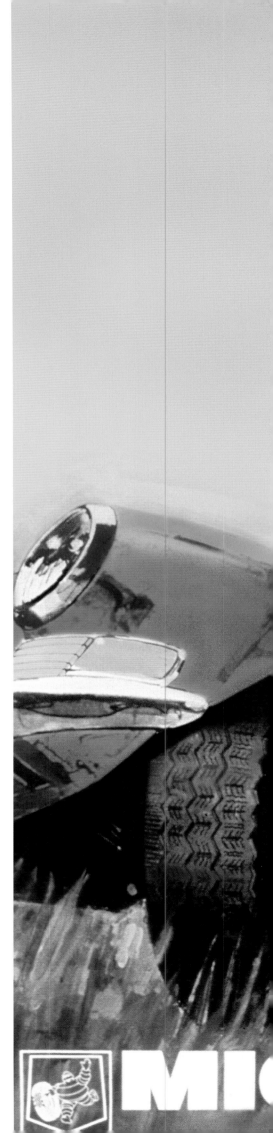

Made for each other !

your imported car and

MICHELIN ZX

The fantastic Formula One Adventure

Three years after this small poster came out announcing Michelin's first victory as formula one world champion with Ferrari, François Michelin visited the Castellet race track in the south of France. His secretary had planned a one-hour visit for him - he ended up staying five! The last of the Formula One stables to be visited was that of McLaren with Niki Lauda, who declared to the eminent visitor: "I've known Firestone, Goodyear and a lot of others, so I can make some comparisons. Your tyres are the best..."

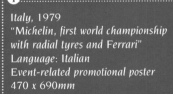

❶ ....

Italy, 1979
"Michelin, first world championship with radial tyres and Ferrari"
Language: Italian
Event-related promotional poster
470 x 690mm

On this Italian poster the rather unusual Bibendum is counterbalanced by Ferrari's famous rearing-horse mascot. Proud of being number one (1979 formula one world champion), Bibendum, graphically speaking, is halfway between the helmeted period of the XAS (1969, page 84) and the front-view "Running Bibendum" to appear in later years.

MICHELIN
il primo radiale
Campione del Mondo
su Ferrari

Lezione di radiale - Checché si dica è Michelin che ha creato il primo "radiale" con cintura stabilizzatrice in fili di acciaio tipo "X" e rivoluzionando l'architettura del pneumatico tradizionale, ha imposto al mondo intero una concezione costruttiva di avanguardia.

Questa tecnica rivoluzionaria è stata infatti seguita dagli altri fabbricanti soltanto 15 anni dopo.

Michelin però, in trent'anni di continue ricerche ed esperienze, ha costantemente perfezionato il "suo" radiale sino a realizzare il radiale per Formula 1.

Oggi, a soli due anni dal suo esordio nelle Competizioni, il pneumatico radiale Michelin si impone anche in F. 1 ed è Campione del Mondo sui rossi bolidi di Maranello.

Oggi Michelin, per la sua incontrastata superiorità, è sempre il "primo" al mondo nel campo del radiale.

Campione del Mondo dei radiali.

Formel 1 1978: 5 sejre for Michelin radialdæk

pa Ferrari med Carlos Reutemann og Gilles Villeneuve

Renault-Turbo und Michelin.
Die neue Formel in der Formel 1.

Vice-Champion du Monde
Alain PROST
Renault - Michelin

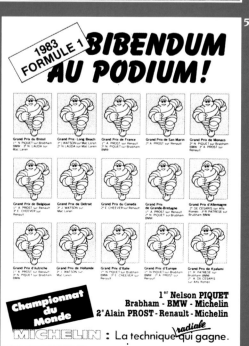

1983 FORMULE 1 BIBENDUM AU PODIUM!

1ᵉʳ Nelson PIQUET
Brabham - BMW - Michelin
2ᵉ Alain PROST - Renault - Michelin

Championnat du Monde

MICHELIN : La technique radiale qui gagne.

2

Denmark, 1978
"1978 Formula One: 5 victories for
Michelin radial tyres, with Ferrari
and racing drivers Carlos Reutemann
and Gilles Villeneuve"
Product presented: Michelin X radial
Language: Danish
610 x 450mm

3

Germany, 1983
"Renault-Turbo and Michelin:
the new formula in Formula One"
Language: German
970 x 690mm

4

France, 1983
"Runner-up to world champion
Alain Prost
Renault-Michelin"
Language: French
800 x 610mm

5

France, 1983
"1983 Formula One
Bibendum on the podium"
Language: French
440 x 610mm

**Bibendum monopolises
victories on the race tracks**

"Do you know why, in 1983, Michelin
was world champion or European
champion in all categories? It's because
the company, for about ten years now,
has men who are capable of defining
objectives, understanding, working
together on a project, and that they do
it better than the others..."
Pierre Dupasquier, head of Michelin's
competitions department during the
great years of formula one.
Another note: Michelin was also formula
one world champion in 1983 with
Brabham-BMW and in 1984 with
McLaren-TAG-Porsche.

The ski resort rush

In the 1970s, the leisure civilisation begins to change from myth to reality, with an explosion in the number of visits to winter resorts. Michelin accompanies this new tendency by designing a poster for its M+S tyre. The idea of a St Bernard saving motorists with tyres around his neck instead of a cask of brandy is a stroke of graphic genius, quite typical of this period. Meanwhile, Bibendum seems to be walking carefully over slippery snow-covered ground, but with no risk of sliding, since he's wearing M+S!

1 ....

France, 1968
"Private car snow tyre
XM+S Michelin"
Language: French
Creation: Michelin Paris Studio
1150 x 1600mm

2

France, 1976
"Michelin M+S radial"
Language: French
Creation: Michelin Paris Studio
640 x 840mm

3

France, 1975
"Michelin XM+S radial"
Language: French
Creation: Michelin Paris Studio
640 x 840mm

When the snow tyre opens up the road

In the late 1960s customers generally began to take an interest in Michelin snow tyres. Other users, true mountain dwellers or those in Northern Europe, had known about the advantages of Michelin snow tyres for a long time. In 1968 comes the XM, the first all-purpose winter tyre with deep treads. A year later comes the XM+S Tourisme. This tyre was designed especially for snow, owing to its deep sipes. The tread ejects snow and because of the alternating positions of the tread blocks the tyre grips well. For over ten years these Michelin tyres were the favourite of winter drivers. As for trucks, the XM+S tyre is conceived for maximum road grip. Virtually all official cars for the 1968 Grenoble Olympic Games, after comparative trials, were equipped with XM+S tyres.

Beach games, ah! the good times

To go and play on the beach without any stress, what better way than by bicycle? Bibendum is on holiday, he is calm, rested...and it's his shadow that smiles. Again an excellent poster from the Michelin Paris Studio.
Every participant in a Michelin beach game receives a three-dimensional puzzle, a modest plastic Bibendum. It is a true brain-teaser which goes together and comes apart... if you understand the trick. Many were they who played for hours with this gadget imagined by Michelin.

❶..................................

France, 1967
"Michelin G.T., new bike tyre"
Language: French
Creation: Michelin Paris Studio
450 x 700mm

❷..................................

France, 1968
"The Big Michelin Game on 4 July at Perros-Guirec"
Language: French
Creation: Michelin Paris Studio
400 x 670mm

Note the "psychedelic" multi-coloured Bibendum. This is one of the rare times when the Michelin Man, usually all in white, dons such a colourful outfit.

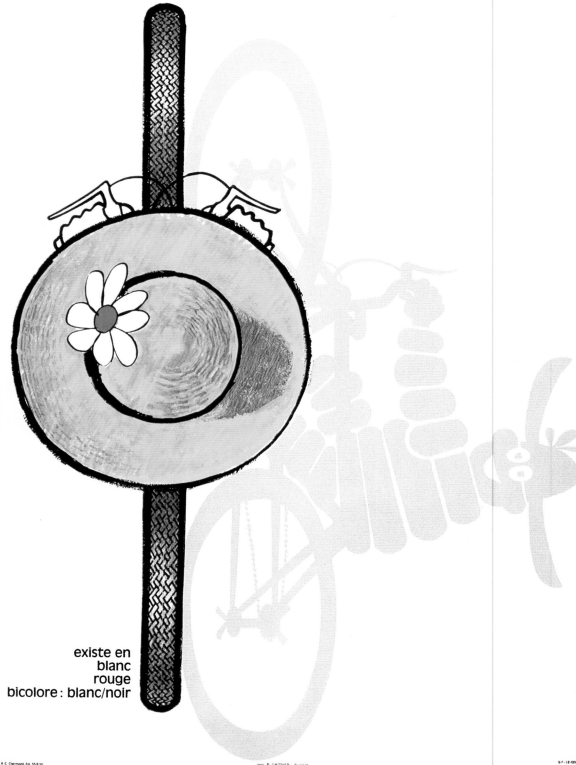

le 4 juillet à Perros-Guirec

**Pour tous les jeunes de 7 à 15 ans
Tout participant gagne un lot**

2

**Jeu
de
plage
MICHELIN**

800 lots par jour

Qui peut participer ? Tous les jeunes de 7 à 15 ans.
Comment participer ? En arrêtant un Bibendum
à parapluie bleu qui se promènera dans votre ville
le matin du jeu. **Sur votre demande** il vous re-
mettra l'"objet Michelin" que vous devrez obliga-
toirement présenter au début du jeu, l'après-midi.

3

4

5

6

3

France
"Michelin Beach Game
800 prizes daily"
Language: French
Event-related promotional poster

4

Germany, 1974
"Great Michelin Game"
Language: German
Event-related promotional poster
400 x 650mm

5

Germany, 1966
"Great Michelin Game"
Language: German
Event-related promotional poster
Creation: Michelin Paris Studio
400 x 630mm

6

Germany, 1972
"Great Michelin Game"
Language: German
Event-related promotional poster
Creation: Michelin Paris Studio
400 x 650mm
Tyres in colour! Could this be a foretaste of
the "Coraldo", the tinted tyre,
commercialised by Michelin in 1996?

Long live the holidays!

Each summer between 1960 and 1980
Bibendum sends news of his stay at the
beach. In Germany, in France and in
Italy young holidaymakers participate
by the thousands in the Michelin beach
games. Traditionally, these promotional
events are organised each afternoon in
a different resort and goodies are
distributed very generously. In 1969 for
example the campaign along the French
Atlantic coast required a team of
36 people, Michelin employees helped
by students and young teachers.
The stars of the show are a
1910 vintage car and fire engine,
and of course the omnipresent
Bibendum, who does not fail to amuse
young and old alike.

The XAS, first asymmetrical tyre

Michelin ran an unusual campaign for an asymmetrical tyre, which would have greatly pleased André Michelin, the "father" of the firm's advertising. To begin with, something absolutely remarkable, a Michelin Paris Studio poster very much in the Pop Art style. One would believe it to be a masterpiece by the great American artist Roy Lichtenstein.

In addition to this internationally distributed image, Michelin launched a campaign based on a very simple drawing: Bibendum is seated, suspended in the air, holding a stylised steering wheel. The impression of speed is created by the disppearing shadows and the slightly slanted French word for speed.

Lastly, one by the master of contemporary posters, Raymond Savignac; here Bibendum fulfils his original purpose again by "giving his body away" to the motorists (see page 85).

1

International, 1965
"XAS Michelin"
Language: French
Creation: Michelin Paris Studio
420 x 600mm

3

2

France, 1968
"Michelin XAS speed"
Language: French
Creation: Michelin Paris Studio
1600 x 690mm

3

France, 1968
"Back of double-decker bus", Paris

Bibendum in Belgium

Michelin is present commercially in Belgium from 1914, with a sales office established in Brussels. As popular as in France, Bibendum is the promotional character who has the strongest immediate recognition in Belgium. When one knows the Belgian fondness for comics and graphics, it is not surprising that Bibendum is appreciated by all Belgian generations, from age 7 to 77...

The XAS, first on the race tracks

At the end of 1967 a competition is created by the French Federation of Sports Cars under the name of "Formule France". The tyre choice can be anything, but they must be in the "private car" category. In Albi, on the 31 March 1968, 15 drivers participate in the first race; only five are on XAS. Result: the first four are on XAS. At Nogaro, two weeks later, there are over twenty competitors. The 20 best qualifying times are on XAS. In the following races, all single-seater vehicles in the Formule France were on ... XAS.

6

France, 1965
"Michelin's new XAS!"
Language: French
Product presented: XAS tyre
Illustration by Raymond Savignac
800 x 1200mm

Raymond Savignac

This artist, born in Paris in 1907, left his mark on the contemporary period of poster art. Even if he did not invent the Michelin promotional image himself, he has the credit of having dared to rethink his role, which at the time seemed set to follow the tried and tested rules of the past. His career is marked by posters for Monsavon, Dunlop, Téfal, Cinzano and the famous "Aspro", where a line of backfiring cars tortures an unfortunate migraine sufferer. Savignac said himself that his credo was: "If I express myself with gags and tricks, if my posters are clownish graphics, it is because the public is terribly bored in its daily routine. I believe that advertising should amuse people."

When the Red Guides go out to dinner

Bibendum pays his bills in the restaurants he recommends, remaining incognito, because in order to retain their credibility, the Red Guide inspectors never make themselves known.
Bibendum must therefore be "satisfied" with promoting his Maps and Guides only where they are sold. Thousands of bookshops regularly distribute the Red Guide each year, as soon as it comes out.
The posters designed for the launch are always in a small format, so that they can be easily placed on a door or in a shop window. The "on sale here" is discreet, but present.

1.....................................

France, 1974
"1974 Guides"
Language: French
Creation: Michelin Paris Studio
300 x 460mm

2.....................................

Great Britain, 1974
"New Michelin Guide to Hotels and Restaurants, Great Britain and Ireland"
Language: English
Creation: Michelin Paris Studio
320 x 490mm

GUIDES 1974
MICHELIN
France / Benelux / Deutschland / España-Portugal
Great-Britain and Ireland / Italia
Camping Caravaning en France

A very special Michelin Map

Bibendum is so confident about the reliability and extreme precision of his Maps that in 1954 he publishes an "Official Map of the Tour de France" in which the off-route part is (quite intentionally) full of mistakes! There were prizes to be won for those who discovered the errors; cars, scooters, lightweight motorcycles, bicycles, etc... tumble from Bibendum's cornucopia.

Above all, don't forget the Guide!

After the Second World War, the Red Guide gradually began to re-award stars to restaurants between 1947 and 1951. It continues to predominate as "the" reference and the attribution of stars remains a press event, while the great majority of faithful "Michelin" motorists continue to frequent less exclusive restaurants. They prefer establishments which are well-run, clean and where they get their money's worth; the type of restaurant which Bibendum recommends by the thousand. France is not alone in having a Red Guide; they are published for Belgium and Luxembourg, Germany, Spain, Portugal, Great Britain, Ireland, Italy and Switzerland.

The radial revolution

The radial pneumatic tyre was to revolutionise the world of motoring. As this poster proclaims, with the Michelin X tyre Bibendum-the-frogman is adding extra kilometres to the tank capacity. For another poster, the X tyre is the triumph of "more" safety, "more" kilometres and "more" petrol savings.

1 ....

France, 1961
"With the Michelin X there are more kilometres in your tank!"
Language: French
450 x 700mm

2 ....

Spain, 1967
"Michelin X is surer, lasts longer and is more economical".
Language: Spanish
500 x 700mm

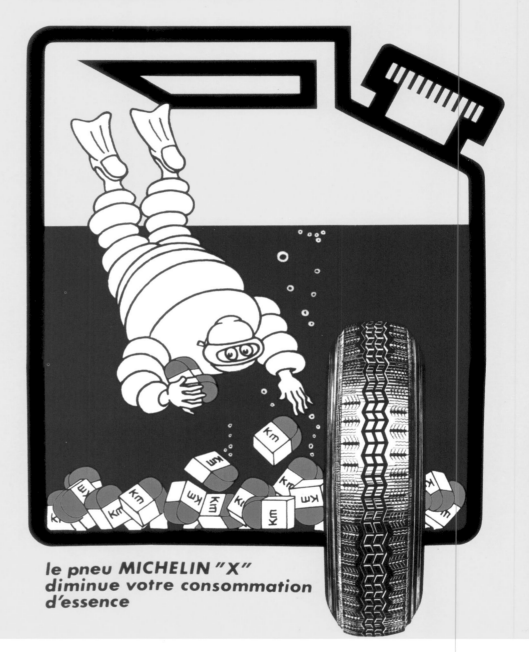

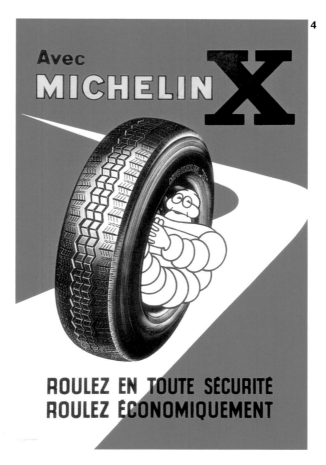

3

The Netherlands, 1961
"Michelin lowers its prices.
Michelin - The highest quality
for the lowest price".
Language: Dutch
450 x 710mm

4

France, 1960
"With Michelin X, drive
with complete safety
Drive economically".
Language: French
760 x 1170mm

5

Morocco, 1958
"Michelin X
Twice as many kilometres"
Language: Arabic and French
Creation: Michelin Paris Studio
790 x 490mm

How the Revolution came about:

Michelin's radial tyre was a veritable technological revolution - which was to be baptised the "X" tyre from 1949. It gradually conquered all types of vehicles and all markets, giving Michelin a decided edge over its competitors until the 1980s. The invention of the "X" tyre, with its "steel belted" radial construction, brought enhanced motoring performance to the entire world. In the new tyre's design, sidewall and tread have clearly distinct independent functions. The basic reinforcement comprises a layer of cords positioned radially to the rolling direction. This was a complete revolution in the technical concept of the tyre, bringing greater comfort, longevity and road grip. After having lodged a patent in 1946, Michelin gradually adapted the "X" tyre to cars (1948), vans (1951), trucks and buses (1953), earthmoving equipment (1955), racing cars (1967), aircraft (1981) and motorcycles (1987).

Life in Yellow and Blue

Three examples of posters from 1950 to 1960. At this time, Bibendum sees everything through yellow and blue glasses. Is this in homage to the colours of his twin home towns Clermont (blue) and Montferrand (yellow)? These colours were already on the Eclair, the first car in the world fitted with detachable tyres, in 1895. Ever since, these colours have been found regularly in Michelin's promotional material.

❶......................................

France, 1952
"Get us to have a look at your worn-out Michelin tyres. They could make good Michelin retreaded tyres".
Language: French
Product presented: Retreads
340 x 570mm

Note the "worn-out" Bibendum on the left, out of action because of the holes in the soles of his shoes!

Faites-nous examiner vos **MICHELIN** usés. Ils peuvent faire de bons rechapés **MICHELIN**

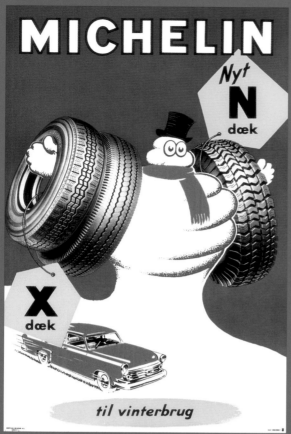

2

Denmark, 1957
"Michelin, new "N" tyre.
X tyres for winter use".
Language: Danish, also
in Finnish and Swedish
Product presented: "X" tyre
450 x 680mm

3

International, 1950
Language: French
Corporate poster
470 x 710mm

Bibendum reclines on a cushion, still
smoking his cigar in 1950. The "smoking
Bib" had disappeared from the Guides in
about 1930... this was probably an
adaptation of an earlier poster.
(See "Superconfort", page 103).

Bibendum
on two wheels

After the Second World War, the bicycle represented a practical, and above all, an economical means of transport. For the following two decades, the motorcycle and the scooter gradually joined the ranks of means of transport, while waiting for the general quality of life to make it possible for more people to put themselves behind the steering wheel of a car. Among the series of posters that vaunted the merits of Michelin "two-wheeler" tyres, this first one, created by the Michelin Paris Studio, is similar to the work of Jean Effel and is typical of the period.

1 ....

France, About 1948
Michelin "Airstop"
"You make me laugh with your records of endurance gliding, my Airstop inner tubes hold their air for more than six months!..."
Language: French
Creation: Jean Mailloux
Product presented: Airstop inner tube
300 x 460mm

Jean Mailloux

Michelin Paris Studio graphic artist, Jean Mailloux, was one of Bibendum's principal creators for almost forty years, especially through the innumerable representations of the Michelin Man peopling the Red and Green Guides. He greatly contributed to Bibendum's popularity by drawing him in virtually all possible situations. It therefore became easy for readers to identify with the Michelin Man.

MICHELIN
scooter

2

France, 1955
"Michelin scooter"
Language: French
Product presented: scooter tyre
Creation: Michelin Paris Studio
390 x 770mm

Bibendum looks so happy to be
driving an attractive and modern
young girl (short skirt and ponytail)
on a beautiful stylised scooter.

It should be noted that the "two-wheeler" Bibendum is always very expressive in his attitudes, and clear about his message. He smiles at the choice of tyres he can put on his bicycle; he sways and climbs uphill (see Tour de France Map page 87) or zooms into the picture on his motorcycle in this colourful poster (opposite).

❸ ....

France, 1951
Language: French
Product presented: Bicycle tyre
350 x 500mm

Bibendum holds his breath!

Butyl rubber, a very airtight material, makes it possible to substantially reduce air loss in tyres. It is used in the 1950s in a new inner tube called "Airstop". In several European countries a number of synthetic rubber factories start producing butyl rubber from petroleum hydrocarbons.

Bibendum upstaged by his product

In the 1930s, Michelin advertising seemed less inspired. André Michelin, the real creator of diversity and audacity in Michelin advertising, died in 1931. After this date, the Michelin Paris Studio produced rather conventional posters, effective, of course, but lacking the vivacity which had characterised the earlier period of Michelin product promotion. As always, some exceptions confirmed the rule. It is notably the case with the poster by Georges Plasse in the line of advertising produced in "L'Illustration" (no 1). His style recalled that of Louis Icart, one of the great engravers of the time. As for colours, Michelin posters from the 1930s are marked by a clear predominance of yellows, ochres, oranges and blacks.

➊

France, 1933
"The same safety on wet ground as on dry, until the tyre wears itself out.
Michelin "Grand tourisme" tyre"
Language: French
Product presented: "Grand tourisme" tyre
Illustration by Georges Plasse
280 x 420mm

MICHELIN [2]

Si vos routes, si votre voiture râpent vos pneus [3]

montez le pneu
MICHELIN
"S"

Le Superconfort "S" est
à lamelles antidérapantes
comme le pneu Stop

En vente ici

MICHELIN [4]

Contre le
dérapage:
les lamelles du pneu
Stop

En vente ici

Contre le dérapage: [5]

le pneu
MICHELIN
Stop
à
lamelles ondulées
qui s'agrippent au sol

MICHELIN [6]
PNEU MOTO

les angles
des nervures
s'accrochent
à la route
et rendent le pneu

parfaitement

antidérapant !

The 1930s, years of decisive progress

Between 1930 and 1939, considerable improvements are made in pneumatic tyre manufacturing. With progress in chemistry helping as well, Michelin launched new products on the market:
1930: patent for the tyre with an integral inner tube, the ancestor of the "tubeless" tyre, and the fine-tuning of the Zig-Zag tread pattern which ensures road grip and reduces noise.
1934: the "Superconfort Stop" introduces adherence sipes that help to reduce the risk of slipping on wet roads.
1937: the creation of the "Pilot" tyre, with a profile that is wider than it is deep. It very much improves road grip at high speed and predates that of the "low-profile" tyres of today.
1938: first tests of the "Métalic", the first tyre for heavy vehicles which combines rubber and steel wire in the casing; these tyres have a much higher resistance to heat and heavy loads. This is an important step in the direction of the later "X" radial tyre. During the Second World War, research in this area continued secretly at Clermont-Ferrand.

7

France, 1934
"The tyre specifically for powerful cars
Michelin "Grand Tourisme" tyre
"The same safety on wet ground as on dry,
until the tyre wears out"
Language: French, also in English
Product presented: "Grand Tourisme" tyre
500 x 1000mm

le pneu spécial pour
voitures puissantes

Grand tourisme
Michelin

se fait dans
les dimensions :

15·45
15·50
16·45
16·50
17·45
17·50
5.50 17
5.50 18
5.50 19
6.00 17
6.00 18
6.00 19
6.00 20
6.00 21
6.50 17
7.00 18
7.00 20
7.00 21

même sécurité
sur sol mouillé que sur sol sec,
jusqu'à usure du pneu

The snow tyre leaves its mark

When, in 1936, Bibendum shows the sole of his hobnailed boots in this poster, he is making an allusion to the strength of the tread, as shown in the 1905 version "Coup de la Semelle" (see page 146)

France, 1936
"The Michelin snow tyre
-eliminates chains
-works well on dry ground.
It is also available in sizes for both cars and trucks"
Language: French
Product presented: Snow tyre.
730 x 1130mm

It was not until 1933 that the first real Michelin snow tyre, the "N" tyre (for "neige", the French word for "snow") appeared. The N tyre had a conventional design, with a massive and deeply cut tread.

The clever butcher-boy

We are in the year 1928. While working in a slaughterhouse, John Sipe, an American butcher, was trying to find a way to stop slipping and falling on the wet floor. After a few fruitless experiments, he hit on the idea of taking his great knife and making several long parallel cuts in the soles of his rubber boots. He immediately stopped slipping...
The Michelin research department registered the first patent in 1930 which consisted of making cuts on the tyre's rolling circumference. This was followed by patents where sipes were included in the tyre manufacturing mould, which created a tyre with a better road grip.

Bibendum
swings
on the green

Bibendum made the decision not to waste his energy by diversifying. Nevertheless, there were several exceptions to this "mono-product" rule. One of them was the golf balls manufactured in England in the 1930s.

An announcement appeared in the 1932 Red Guide to France, stating: "The Michelin golf ball is perfectly balanced, travels far, is very resistant to cuts, and is worthy of the best players". The English poster vaunting these golf balls is particularly interesting because of its elaborate design of intersecting circles in various sizes and colours. Note the drawing of Bibendum, a simple silhouette on one poster, while on the other he wears a natty pair of the two-tone golf shoes so fashionable at the time.

① International, 1932
"Michelin golf ball"
Language: English
600 x 420mm

② France, 1932
"On French golf courses use
the Michelin golf ball"
Language: French
380 x 580mm

③ France, 1934
"Michelin Sports Articles:
All types of ball
at the lowest prices"
Language: French
240 x 500mm

A certain return to the beginnings

It was because of bouncing balls that the ultimate establishment of Michelin at Clermont-Ferrand began, in 1832, with Messrs Barbier and Daubrée. The story of this rubber industry's development in the heart of France is full of interesting details. Edouard Daubrée saw his wife playing with a rubber ball, which made him think of replacing the leather agricultural pump seals with ones made of rubber. Madame Elizabeth Daubrée, née Pugh Barker, is the niece of MacIntosh, the English manufacturer who, in 1823 found a way to make fabric impermeable by coating it with rubber dissolved in benzine.
- In 1889, the Michelin brothers took over the factory that belonged to Aristide Barbier, their grandfather. In the 1930s, a century after the first rubber balls were manufactured in Clermont-Ferrand, these modest leisure toys were re-launched, to be greatly appreciated by Bibendum and all the family.

Prudent advice

Throughout the century, Michelin remained particularly attentive to motorists' safety, as well as that of cyclists and of course children. To promote road safety, the Michelin Paris Studio used the comic strip technique with captions, as on this poster signed by Jean Mailloux. The style recalls another artist of the period who also drew children (such as the turbulent Quick and Flupke): a certain Georges Rémy, alias "Hergé", creator of Tintin.

France, 1932
"Watch out!"
Language: French
350 x 550mm

Une révolution!

Dans un Fauteuil
.......".à pleins gaz"
sur mauvaises routes

avec
le pneu

SUPERCONFORT
MICHELIN

gonflé
de 1 kg. à 1 kg. 400

Bibendum, in an armchair

The Michelin Paris Studio began producing its first photomontages for the "Superconfort" posters. The contrast is flagrant between the impression of the car's speed on the rough cobblestones and the transfer drawing of Bibendum, comfortably settled in an armchair. The overall result is very much to the point. The idea of putting Bibendum in an armchair or on a cushion will be taken up in various forms after the War.

MICHELIN
Superconfort
gonflé de 0ᵏᵍ9 à 1ᵏᵍ8
Confort parfait - Sécurité absolue

❶

France, 1932
"A revolution! In an armchair...
with the throttle open" on a poor road
with a Michelin "Superconfort" tyre
(which is inflated from 1kg to 1.4kg
instead of from 2kg to 2.25kg).
Language: French, also in German

❷

France, 1934
"Michelin "Superconfort", inflated from
0.9kg to 1.8kg
Perfect comfort - Absolute safety"
Language: French
500 x 1000mm

Bibendum
on rails

In about 1930 Bibendum noted: "We have already seen the pneumatic tyre completely change automotive transport; we thought that it could perhaps do the same thing for rail transport". As soon as the innovation is realised and then adopted by the railway companies, this advertisement is published to inform the public of free demonstrations organised to promote "the Michelin-tyre rail-car" that the "vox populi" soon calls the "Micheline".

Allez essayer la
"MICHELINE"

**Premier auto-rail sur pneus
créé par Michelin**

*Démonstrations organisées
par les Chemins de fer de l'EST*

15 et 16 Septembre
entre **Épinal, Vittel** et **Contrexéville**

17 et 18 Septembre
entre **Épinal** et **Gérardmer**

1-13-458-9-310.5   R.C. Clermont-Ferrand n° 2.213

1

France, 1931
"Go test the "Micheline"
First rail-car on tyres created by Michelin"
Demonstration organised by Eastern
Railways...
Language: French
320 x 510mm

France, 1950
"Always in the vanguard of progress
Michelin has created the Métro
tyre for you"
Language: French
Corporate poster - Métro tyre

2

From the Micheline to the Métro on tyres

Travelling on the Micheline is a sensation so far quite unknown on the railway system. The excellent grip of the tyre to the rail makes it possible to stop in under a 100 metres (as opposed to 1 000 metres for a conventional train); it is now also possible to reach speeds of 80km an hour in 600m (as opposed to 1 500m for a conventional train). The 125 rail-cars manufactured by Michelin run on several lines in France as well as in the French colonies, but also on certain European networks until the 1950s. After the Micheline the next field of development will be the Métro tyre... Underground trains running on pneumatic tyres began on 13 April 1952. Since this date, more than 3 000 such trains run on Michelin tyres, in Montreal, Mexico and in Santiago (1967-1973), as in Marseilles, Lyon, Toulouse, Orlyrail and Lille. The next step forward is tramway networks for trams on tyres (particularly in Clermont-Ferrand, France). This will be for the beginning of the 21st century...

1936

Travelling with Bibendum's advice

Every year, Michelin produces small posters for bookshops to announce the arrival of the Red Guide. They are logically in red tones and clearly and naturally show off the guides they are meant to promote.
In 1926 another collection of Guides is born, devoted to the regions of France and which provides the itinerary advice which had been offered for free to motorists since 1908 by the Michelin Tourism Office. These regional Guides put the accent on the curiosities and sights to visit. Also red, they progressively cover all France's regions. In the late 1930s they changed colour, to distinguish them from the Hotel Guide; these were to become the famous "Green Guides".
On all these posters, Bibendum, dressed as a master chef or in regional costume, is the one who invites the reader to travel, to make the touristic or gastronomic discovery.

1 ....

France, 1932
"1932 Guide"
Language: French
250 x 400mm

2 ....

Belguim, 1936
"Guide 1936-1937"
Language: French
250 x 400mm

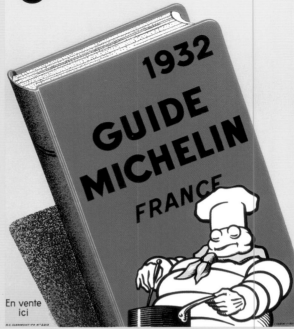

The Red Guide and its vocation

Up until 1920 the Red Guide's 17 annual editions (it does not appear from 1915 to 1918) are distributed for free each spring. The Guide is the privileged companion of all those France considers to be the "gentleman" driver. Its reputation is reinforced by Michelin's Road Maps, launched in 1910. After the Great War, the French begin to get "itchy feet". Bibendum decides to recommend restaurants in its Guide to help these new travellers. Therefore, the Guide renounces all forms of paid additions to its text - a decision that has been respected up to today (and not without a certain degree of pride...). This is what partly explains, no doubt, its image of independence. 1926 sees the creation of the "Stars for Fine Dining", meant to make known the chefs' talents and to distinguish the best among them. In 1931 came the creation of two or three Stars in the provinces. It wasn't until 1933 that three Stars appeared in Paris.

The Aviation Guide

"The first guide for touristic aviation...and it's a Michelin Guide..." With this new product, Bibendum is once more a forerunner, at the height of a period very much marked by aviators' exploits, from Lindbergh to Saint-Exupéry and not forgetting Mermoz, Costes, Bellonte, etc...After a quarter of a century, Bibendum raises his arm and seems to recall his efforts already on behalf of aviation (see page 139). This poster has a somewhat Art Deco look to it, as seen by the stylised aircraft silhouettes. Its blue, of course, evokes the colours of the sky, of azure, while also making a point of avoiding confusion with the other Michelin Guides.

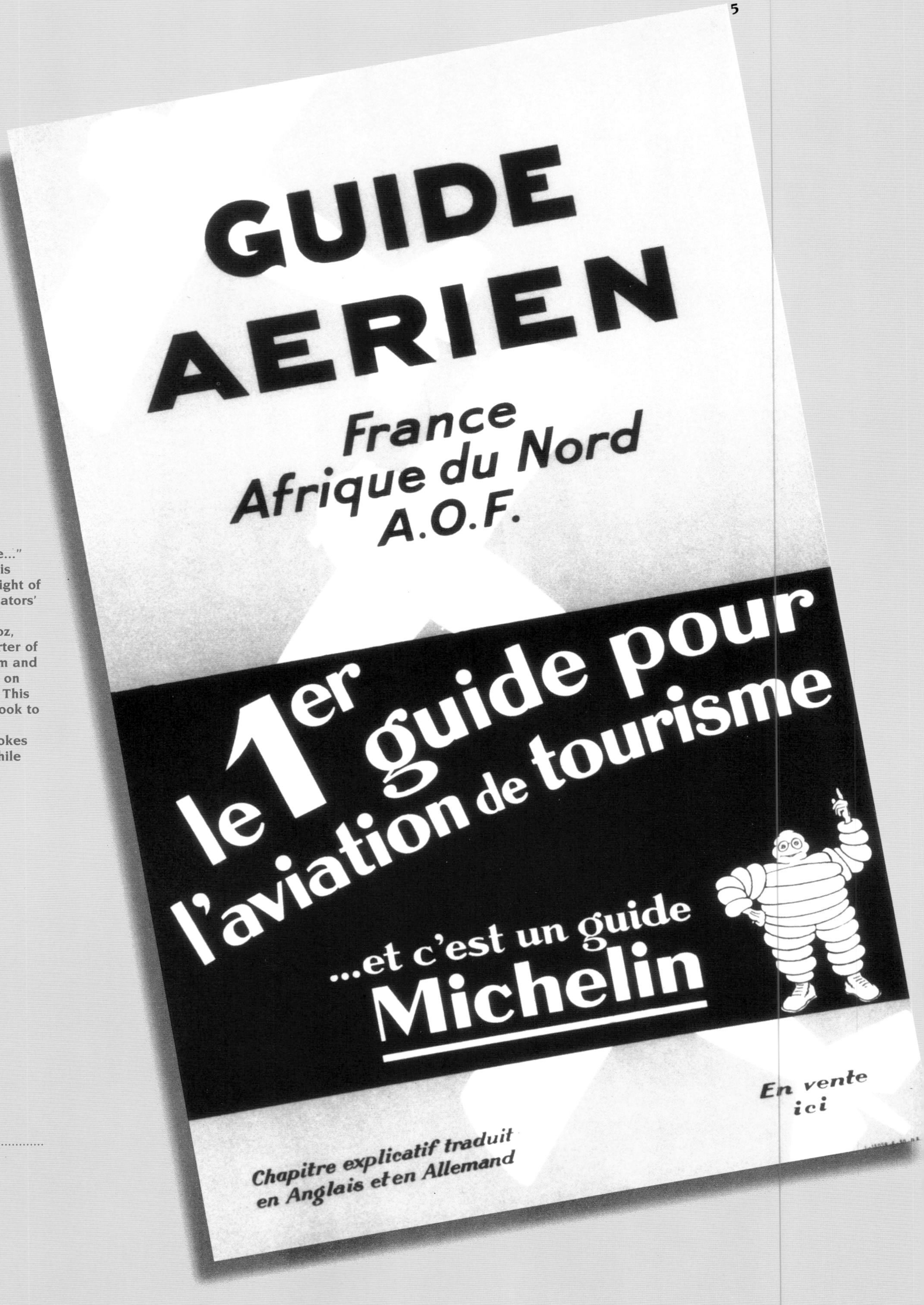

5

France, 1930
"Aerial Guide
France - North Africa -
French West Africa"
Language: French
240 x 400mm

Bibendum and Automotive Transport

Attentive to the development of motor vehicle traffic, in the 1930s Bibendum publishes a "timetable for road freight". The poster has rather surprising contrasts: on the one hand, the conventional look to the typeface, barely altered by the two last lines on a slight curve; and on the other hand a heavily loaded Bibendum running down parallel grey lines evoking a road. The most interesting part of the poster, however, is in its shadow: on the lower left, the purplish tones barely differentiate a highly stylised Art Deco tree, somewhat in the manner of Raoul Dufy.

France, 1932
"Michelin Timetable!"
Language: French
Product presented: Guides
250 x 400mm

Information at "the right time"

Anxious to provide their motorist friends with up-to-date and accurate information, Michelin edited a series of maps called "State of the Roads" between 1929 and 1935 which classified French roads according to the quality of the surface: Good; tar, cobblestone - Good; not tarred - Average; bulging tar - Bad - Very bad. These maps were updated three times each year so as to highlight the major road works planned for the network.

They were followed by leaflets, "Fast Roads" (1935-1939), which principally identified, for the benefit of long-distance drivers, roads with even and uneven surfaces as well as indicating the 24hr petrol stations.

In 1945 Michelin likewise edited a map called "Roads and Bridges", which marked the roads that had been damaged or destroyed during the war.

7

France, 1933
"To avoid roads in a bad condition, Michelin map State of the Roads".
Language: French
250 x 500mm

When Bibendum shows the way...

The creation of Michelin's Itinerary Office in 1908 and the company's campaign to number the roads (1912), were decisive actions on the part of Bibendum to promote motor vehicle traffic and tourism. On a simple request, be it for business trips, outings or holidays, Michelin's Parisian service indicated the best itinerary by return post. This Office is the ancester of Bibendum's telematic and Internet services today, but the principle remains the same: to advise and assist the motorist to make his daily life a little easier and to make travels safer, cheaper and more pleasant. Very much in his "yellow and blue" colours, a joyous Bibendum dances here around the globe, in the spirit of the early 1920s.

8

8

France, 1923
"For your business trips, your outings, your holidays".
Language: French
520 x 700mm

Bibendum, Europe's adviser

Despite the rise of the motor-car in the 1920s in Europe and the United States, an entire generation of first-time drivers did not know much about the technical constraints of how much weight the motor-car was bearing and how to maintain the tyres. Therefore Bibendum began to give advice to his friends on the road. Via his posters he informed beginners of all necessary information "so that a tyre provides long service"...: "in advance, calculate the maximum weight to be carried on each axle", and "know in advance how to inflate the tyres correctly according to the weight to be borne".

This Michelin Paris Studio's poster is interesting; it includes no less than 44 representations of the Michelin Man - which is no doubt a record! It should be noted that most of the posters presented in this chapter have been translated into several languages, sometimes as many as a dozen, especially for Northern and Eastern European countries.

1 ....

France, 1922
"So that a tyre provides long service...
1. Do not overload it...
2. Inflate the tyres correctly..."
Language: French
550 x 800mm

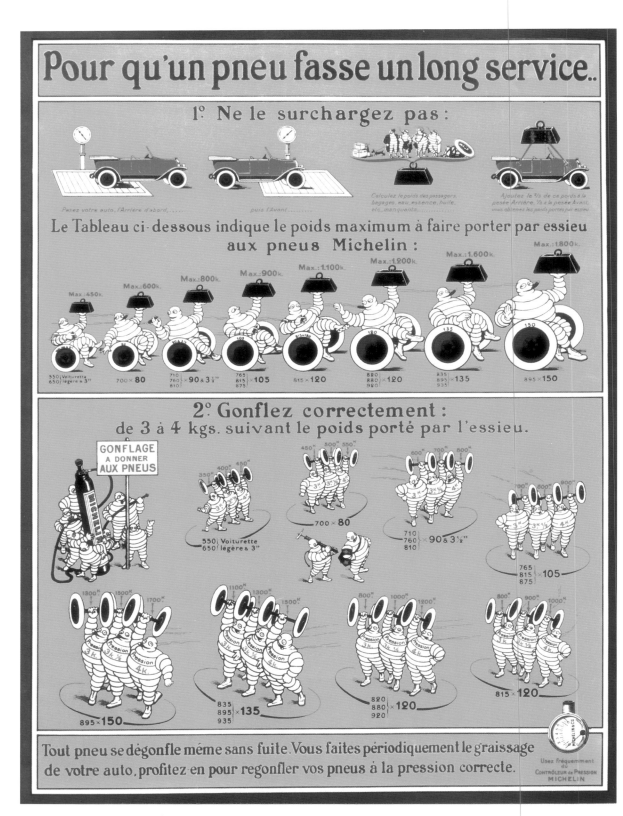

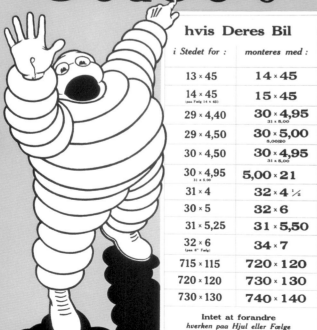

1928

The birth of Bibendum running with his tyre

Bibendum "running with his tyre" is certainly the most famous corporate representation of the Michelin Man. He has illustrated millions of Maps and Guides for decades and has been the logo used on an innumerable number of documents. The first known representation that was a forerunner to "Bib with his tyre" is certainly this poster by Albert Philibert. Taking up a theme which is to recur many times in the future, Bibendum runs across the globe while pushing a tyre with his right hand, the left one raised to wave to his friends. The next year, 1926, a logo displaying the same characteristics appeared on the cover of the Red Guide. And he has remained there for 70 years!

❶

France, 1925
Language: French
Corporate poster
770 x 1120mm

VUE DE L'ATELIER DE RECAOUTCHOUTAGE

2

View of a retreading workshop, about 1925
On the wall, the first poster of
"Bibendum with his tyre"
Postcard, without editor's name

Comfort takes priority

This unsigned poster exists in a French as well as in an English version. It shows Bibendum running, his arms outstretched as he carries a tyre in front of him; in the background, smokestacks are spewing out thick smoke. The black with the strong yellow, along with the red sky over the factories, together create a rather serious mood...The second poster, in English as well, has often been reproduced. It features Bibendum, his arms outstretched in front of him, holding a pile of tyres that are flying off over his head. The colours, from burgundy to yellow, are also particularly striking.

1 ....

France, 1926
"The new Michelin Confort-Bibendum tyre"
(comfort in English)
Language: French, also in English
with the title: "Michelin's British factory
springing up!"
Presented product: "Confort" tyre
1260 x 2000mm

2 ....

United Kingdom, 1927
Language: English
Product presented: Comfort tyre, trefoil
tread pattern
890 x 760mm

American comfort

This poster is probably the first advertisement combining a photomontage and a drawn Bibendum. Printed in France, it was meant for the United States, Brazil and Argentina, Ford's main customer markets. Bibendum presents a Ford motor-car here.

Fit 730×130 MICHELIN "COMFORT" and make your FORD look and ride like a car "de luxe"

Standard Ford Saloon fitted with 730×130 "Comforts".

Michelin Tire Co., Milltown, N. J.

1

United States, 1925
"Fit 730 x 130 Michelin "Comfort" and make your Ford look and ride like a car "de luxe" (sic)
Language: English, Portuguese, Spanish
Product presented: "Comfort" tyre
890 x 760mm

2

United States, 1928
Postcard
The Michelin factory in Milltown, New Jersey, was built in 1908. Michelin's idea was to manufacture near the Ford factories, to serve this major customer with tyres for the new cars as efficiently as possible. Milltown closed its doors in 1931, with the great economic crisis of the Depression.

Bibendum plays up to the camera

In 1925, Bibendum explains *"that by a simple discovery, the result of a well-organised analysis and summary, all the qualities that we desire for the pneumatic tyre are reaffirmed. Due to a clever device, it is absolutely impossible that the Bibendum Confort tyre can come off while the vehicle is moving, however slow or fast that may be, and yet no operation could be simpler than that of removing or fitting the tyre".*
To prove his know-how, Bibendum decided to use the cinema and he gave the public an interesting sample of this "new art" (new for the period) with free showings of a filmed demonstration. In France, Michelin tried to show how its new tyre could not possibly come off by itself; in Great Britain, Bibendum referred to the studies done on the Comfort by filming a glass of milk set on the running-board while the motor-car went over a thick wooden plank! These films still exist in the company's archives and are full of information on the extent of imagination used since the beginning by the research department.

❶...

France, 1928
*"Cinéma -
Motorists!
Go and see the Michelin film on the new Bibendum "Confort" tyre, which will be at...."
Language: French
Product presented: "Confort" tyre
400 x 600mm*

Cinéma

Automobilistes!
Allez voir le film
MICHELIN
sur le nouveau pneu
CONFORT-BIBENDUM

il passera
à

2

Great Britain, 1926
"The tyre has made it to the cinema,
the astounding tests filmed by the
Michelin Research Centre"
Language: English
Corporate poster
2000 x 1500mm

Uncommon transport

This poster was part of an especially successful humorous series. A 1924 Michelin public relations campaign attacked the last bastions of the solid tyre: the Paris motor-coach. Bibendum used the "rebound" technique of putting pressure on the Parisian area public transport companies by getting the customers on his side. Isn't the humour contagious? The push is on the Paris bus users to "claim equality of treatment", by reminding them that "pigs are transported on pneumatic tyres and not on solid ones", like wine or villains in a Black Maria, while Parisians still get around in buses with solid tyres. It is expensive for the passengers and they reach their destination like sardines.

Parisiens ! Un scandale :

Les cochons sur pneus,

Vous, sur bandages pleins !

Réclamez l'égalité de traitement !

I ....

France, 1924
"Parisians! A scandal"
Language: French
Corporate poster
400 x 310mm

SERVICE D'AUTOMOBILES

Lignes de

CLERMONT-FERRAND à:

Thiers
Billom
Champeix
Vic=le=Comte
Saint=Amant=Tallende

Demander l'horaire au Bureau de l'Hôtel ou au Bureau du Service d'Automobiles, Place Gaillard, à **CLERMONT**-FERRAND.

IMPRIMERIE CHAIX, rue Bergère, 20, Paris. — 12836-6-13.   1599-6-13. — 5

A few years earlier, Michelin was already thinking about public transport and was experimenting in the region around Clermont-Ferrand with new ideas such as the twinned wheel, created in 1908 for motor-coaches and heavy vehicles. They were first put in pairs in case of a flat. Later, by generally putting twinned wheels on the back of heavily loaded vehicles, it was found to be possible to increase significantly the load being supported by the axle. This is why, confident of his vehicle, Bibendum can guarantee a very stylish welcome for his elegant customers.

②

*France, 1913
"Motor-car service,
Service from Clermont-Ferrand to:
Thiers, Billom, Champeix, Vic-le-Comte,
Saint-Amant-Tallende"
Language: French
Corporate poster
300 x 400mm*

To live happily – let us live "cabled"

At the beginning of the 1920s, Michelin is already present in most European markets; but the posters for internal use promoting the "Cable" (cord casing) tyre and the "Cable Mixte" are also planned for eleven countries of the Old World. On the second poster, Bibendum is like a one-man band; he recalls three facts: Michelin created the motor-car tyre in 1895 (barely 30 years before); he has specialised in tyres; and he has remained the leader in progress...

Upon reflection, this message could practically be used, just as it stands, today! Here is what we could call the longevity in communication, which can be translated better as constancy in a firm's values...

❶ ....

France, 1923
"No flats, no slips
with the new Michelin "Cable Mixte" tyre
on sale here"
Language: French, also in English, Polish,
Spanish, German, Portuguese, Dutch,
Czech, Romanian, Danish and Swedish
Product presented: "Cable" tyre - made
with a cord casing
560 x 730mm

Ni crevaisons,
ni dérapages,
avec le
NOUVEAU PNEU MICHELIN
"CABLÉ-MIXTE"

en vente ici

AFFICHE D'INTERIEUR   PRINTED IN FRANCE

France, 1924
"Michelin tyres on sale here
for all motor-cars"
Language: French, also in English,
Spanish, German, Portuguese, Dutch,
Danish, Swedish
Product presented: "Cable" tyre
560 x 730mm

Czechoslovakia, circa 1920
Michelin's promotions also take place in the
open as with the public relations parade
photographed in Czechoslovakia.
Note the two posters for
the Cable Mixte tyre.

A shop in Lyon where Michelin Cable tyres
are sold in the 1920s, with a veritable tribe
of Bibendums in the windows.

When the Cable tyre holds the reins

Bibendum explains this new progress in
the following way: "An ordinary fabric is
a plaiting, a crosshatch of elements
passing over each other alternately at
right angles. In the criss-cross canvas,
as we call it, of the old tyre
construction, the threads repeatedly
flex over each other; which in turn
means that they get heated and worn
thereby increasing the risk of failure. In
the "Cable" tyre, the warp is no longer
made of individual threads but of cord
and the weave is reduced to being
made of no more than fine threads
spaced as far apart as possible.
Therefore, with elementary reasoning,
we can affirm that it deteriorates much
less quickly than its predecessor and
that in the general propulsion of the
vehicle, it reduces fuel consumption".

Bibendum with wings on his heels

This period begins with these "detachable steel wheel" posters, which we could call the "classic and artistic period" of the Bibendum poster. Printed for the most part by chromolithography, the posters presented in the following pages are contemporary with the works of Chéret, Mucha, Toulouse-Lautrec and many other great artists.

With its orange and red tones, this poster signed "Grand Aigle" (his real name being Henri Genevrier) recalls the period's taste for Greek mythology. This evocation of the God Hermes, protector of travellers and merchants, runs, or rather flies above a detachable wheel. This image, something of a forerunner for the "Bibendum running with his tyre", is placed in a strongly symbolic context. He has indeed just passed a country fellow who has been knocked flying by a kick from his donkey. Without doubt, the detachable wheel signifies here the end of traction by animals, slow and uncertain as it is. Dramatised by curious theatrical lighting, Bibendum can therefore "take flight" towards the future, absorbing the shock of obstacles, accompanied by his faithful dog made of tyres (certainly baptised Bibendog!) - a zoological exception in the kingdom of Bibendum!

1 ....

France, 1925
Language: French
Illustration: Grand Aigle
450 x 650mm

-1-4-167-4-238-   IMP. KARCHER PAR 5   MADE IN FRANCE

MICHELIN

Four years earlier, Albert Philibert had signed this excellent composition, also for the Michelin detachable wheel. The choice of dramatising the situation seems to be the artist's intention from the start. By playing with the chiaroscuro of night driving, Philibert shows a motor-car disappearing into a night which is dark and luminous at the same time, on a road bordered by threatening trees. The foreground shows the back of the vehicle strongly lit and thus shows a reassuring Bibendum, who seems to say: "No problem, we have here with us a detachable steel wheel fitted with a Cable tyre". The open touring-car is being driven (on the right?) by another Bibendum of whom we only see the head and shoulders.

2

France, 1921
Language: French
Illustration: Albert Philibert

A solid disc of steel

Bibendum simplifies the motorist's life in 1913 by launching a detachable steel wheel. This replaced the detachable rim in common use at the time and is the forerunner of the spare wheel and tyre assembly which we know today. Consisting of a standard rim and a pressed steel disc riveted in its centre, this wheel can be changed in a few minutes. It supersedes the old models in wood or even the type with metal spokes which break and become "pockets of mud", impossible to clean. The publicity in the early 1920s period adds: "the steel wheel corresponds perfectly to the beautifully streamlined coachwork".

In the Fabiano style

This poster, of which we know of three versions, shows a modern (for the period!) young woman in the foreground holding a tyre and its inner tube. Behind her stands a protective Bibendum who seems to say, "it's easy with my tyres", with the understanding that "even women can do it". Youth, fashion, comfort, ease of use: a multiple message that must "hit the bull's eye"! The lower part of the poster, left blank on purpose, is the place to put typographic lettering with the name and address of a local seller of the tyre. This image, created against a green background, marks a break because it is the last time we see Bibendum dressed with his laced brown boots. After the War, at the same time as the tyre grows lighter becomes less heavy, he will switch his boots for the classic white ones with which we know him today.

❶..

France, 1916
"Michelin bicycle tyre"
Language: French
Illustration: Fabiano
800 x 1200mm

Although during the First World War publicity was practically non-existent in France, this was not the case in Great Britain where fierce competition demanded the continuation of a commercial presence; this was also the case in the Netherlands, a country which remained neutral during the conflict.

2

The Netherlands, 1917
"Michelin bicycle tyres"
Language: Dutch
Illustration: Fabiano
800 x 1200mm

3

Great Britain
"Michelin cycle cover"
Language: English
Illustration: Fabiano
800 x 1200mm

Fabien Fabiano

This was the pseudonym for Marie Jules Coup de Frejac (1882-1962): French humorous painter and designer, he popularised a type of charming young Parisian girl of the Belle Epoque, known as a "fabianette". He participated in the exhibitions at the Palais des Glaces in Paris, signed several strip cartoons, illustrated numerous works and collaborated regularly with publications such as: Baïonnette, Elegante Welt, Fantasio, Froufrou, l'Intransigeant, Life, La Nation, Paris-Soir, Le Rire, Sans-Gêne, etc.
In advertising, Fabiano is best known for his drawings for Moët & Chandon champagne and various catalogues for Parisian department stores.

1913

1916

Eternal Russia

Even though recently Michelin has opened a sales branch in Moscow (July 1997), the company has been present in Russia since the beginning of the automobile with an establishment at St Petersburg (1913-1917) and in Moscow (1914-1917).
Tsar Nicholas II himself drove Michelin from 1905...
With this poster, René Vincent, one of the automobile world's great illustrators as well as being recognised more generally in advertising, gives back to Bibendum his original function: to put his tyres (of which he is made) in the motorist's service. Doesn't he do so himself, physically, with his very person? It is also interesting to note the portrait of the period's motorist: a man of quality, accompanied by his elegantly dressed spouse, while the children in their patent leather shoes watch with surprise while "good fairy" Bibendum accomplishes his miraculous intervention...

1 ....

Russia, 1914
Language: Russian
Corporate poster
600 x 800mm

2

France, 1914
Language: French
Corporate poster
600 x 800mm

René Vincent

René Vincent Rageot (1879-1936), architectural student at the Beaux-Arts School in Paris (which was frequented, before him, by Edouard and André Michelin) drew many posters and publicity leaflets, particularly for Bugatti, Peugeot and Viator. Very close to the automobile world, he had a great passion for competitions and the development of tourism. An author-illustrator of many works, René Vincent also collaborated with the press: Fantasio, Je sais tout, Lecture pour tous, Nos loisirs, Le Rire, La Vie Parisienne, etc.

pposer qu'à l'intérieur du Magasin
fance et dans les Colonies françaises

When "poulbot" changes a tyre

This composition was meant to de-dramatise a flat tyre, one of the motorist's main apprehensions at the beginning of the century. This same year of 1913, at the Salon de l'Auto, Michelin had a tyre changed by a little girl from Auvergne - what better demonstration of simplicity?

Francisque Poulbot, the father of the famous "Montmartre street urchins" who bear his name, signs here one of his best publicity posters done for Michelin. Under the admiring gaze of his little friends, the "poulbot" at work seems to be quite proud of himself.

Already master of his quite characteristic style, the man who sang of the street children left no detail to chance; such as the small girl who holds a little cloth doll behind her back - a Bibendum complete with cigar! This poster exists also in French, Russian, Danish, Hungarian, Portuguese, Czech, Dutch, Swedish and Austrian. It was the first true pneumatic tyre campaign conducted on a European scale.

❶..

Spain, 1913
"Even a child can change a pneumatic effortlessly..."
Language: Spanish
Illustration: Francisque Poulbot
590 x 800mm

Czechoslovakia, 1913
"Even a child can change
a pneumatic effortlessly..."
Language: Czech
Illustration: Francisque Poulbot
590 x 800mm

Denmark, 1913
"Even a child can change
a pneumatic effortlessly..."
Language: Danish
Illustration: Francisque Poulbot
590 x 800mm

Poulbot in detail

Interviewed by a journalist late in his life, Francisque Poulbot (1873-1946) explained what he saw as his vocation: "I have drawn children all my life because I drew what I knew well and what I loved well". In about 1900, Poulbot settled in the "Maquis", a grouping of poor properties clinging to the side of the Montmartre butte, where artists and totters lived. At the time the quarter was frequented by artists such as Willette and Stenlen, writers such as Courteline, MacOrlan, Dorgelès and songwriters of whom the most famous remains Aristide Bruant.
The free-and-easy way of life on the "Butte" left its mark on the young Poulbot and inspired him to make many drawings which appeared in the highly satirical magazine, "L'Assiette au Beurre", from 1903 to 1910. It is from this period that the "Poulbot" style began and which would never leave him. His work is composed of numerous posters and, above all, postcards by the dozens, which have been around France and even the world thousands of times in the form of correspondence.

Bibendum and the Press

At the same time as the poster, the other major advertising medium from the beginning of the century is of course the press. In France, Michelin singled out magazines targeting the upper classes, such as the weekly magazine "L'Illustration", and monthly reviews, namely "Lectures Pour Tous" and "Je Sais Tout'.

Bibendum likes to demonstrate, drawing upon 1900 humour, the faultless superiority of the Michelin tyre and its technical advance over its competitors. One of his favourite expressions of the time was "Michelin makes tyres, still more tyres, forever tyres…", an affirmation often completed by the strict rule "Only one tyre quality, the best". This single product strategy has been company policy throughout the development of the motor car.

1 ....

France, 1914
The back cover of
"La Petite Illustration"
dated 4 April 1914
Illustration by E.L. Cousyn
Entitled "My Factories",
three Bibendums (representing
the Michelin factory in
Clermont-Ferrand,
the Turin factory supplying Fiat and
the American plant supplying Ford)
deliver quality tyres worldwide
200 x 295mm

1

America, 1920
*In this poster which appeared in
the 21 August 1920 edition of
"The Saturday Evening Post", Bibendum is
established as the motorist's benefactor,
on the 25th anniversary of the invention
of the pneumatic tyre. He reminds us in
passing that he manufactures cord tyres in
Milltown, New Jersey (see page 117).
240 x 315mm*

Bibendum hands out maps

After considerable preparatory work, 1910 saw the appearance of the Michelin road maps, the very first designed for motorists. Great thought and care was given to make them legible and easy to use and "only information relevant to motorists was included, colour was introduced and the maps were presented in a handy folded version".

The series, at a scale of 1:200 000, began on the shores of the Mediterranean and worked northwards.
By 1913 the whole of France was covered by 47 sheet maps. The 48th map, covering the newly liberated regions of Alsace and Lorraine, was published in 1919.

From 1920 onwards maps of Belgium, Switzerland, the British Isles, Italy and Spain were published: the beginnings of a European road network as seen by Michelin!
The years 1921 to 1922 saw the appearance of several detailed maps of the East Coast of America.

❶
....
France, 1919
"La Petite Illustration" 18 October 1919
Bibendum presents his road maps with the help of drawings and captions. He reminds us of the amount of work involved in preparing the maps and underlines the fact that they are both road and tourist maps.
200 x 295mm

❷
....
Bibendum wishes motorists a "safe journey"
Drawing by Hautot
("La Petite Illustration", 10 April 1920)

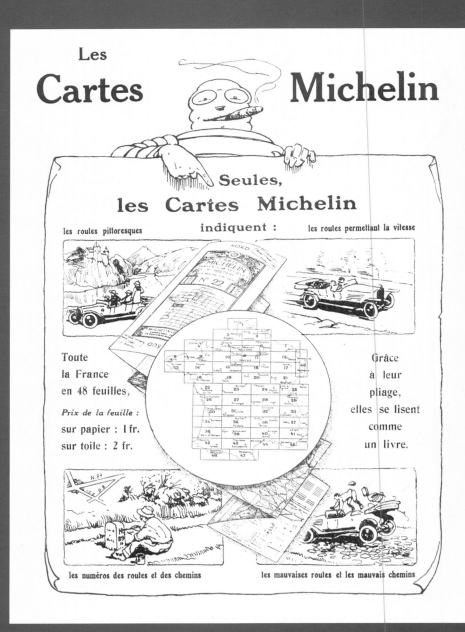

"La Petite Illustration" 24 August 1912
Bibendum proudly reviews Michelin's
various initiatives to encourage automobile
tourism (drawing by Cousyn)
200 x 295mm

Bibendum and the period after the boneshaker

Before 1914, when there is only a small number of motor-cars on our roads, bicycles can be counted in the hundreds of thousands.
The Tour de France inspires the crowds and the bicycle tyre market explodes.
Bibendum was even more readily interested in the demise of the boneshaker as the detachable tyre for two-wheelers was the future.
This series of posters is very much characteristic of the period before 1914.
Whether due to the talents of the Frenchman O'Galop or to that of the Englishman Stanley Roowles, they bear the same message: the Michelin bicycle tyre - the best, for less. It appeared in two colours, blue and yellow. And then, of course, three different poses with Bibendum quite at ease on his bicycle:

- three-quarters view from the front, riding from left to right and distributing his tyres (a gesture taken up by René Vincent in his 1914 poster, Page 128),

- three-quarters view from the front, pedalling jovially from right to left, smoking his cigar, his hand in his left pocket,

- going from right to left, one leg on the handlebars to show a perfectly mastered sense of balance.

1

2

6

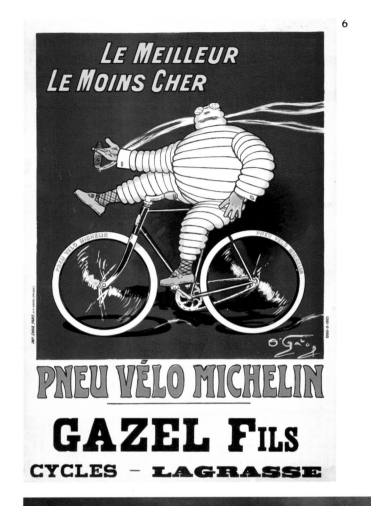

7

6

France, 1911
"The best. The least expensive"
Michelin bicycle tyre'
Language: French
Illustration: O'Galop

Personalised: "Gazel and
Sons Bicycles - Lagrasse"

7

circa 1913
Photograph showing the interior
of a bar with two Michelin bicycle
posters behind the counter

8

France, 1913
"The best. The least expensive.
Michelin bicycle tyre"
Language: French
Not signed
700 x 1150mm

The only exception to the dominant blue
and yellow of the day, this unsigned poster
in black, yellows and reds shows Bibendum
on a bicycle, seen three-quarters from the
back, as a "sandwich-board man". To the
right, the milestone is a direct allusion to
the "Petition to Number the Roads",
launched with success by Michelin
in October 1912. Hence, the satisfied
expression on Bibendum's face, sure
of his tyres and of his road - a double
message for the same poster,
an exceptional step for the period!

Bibendum and Columbine

The Michelin Man carries off a young woman under the amused gaze of the moon and crosses a field of melons protected by bell jars, without taking any great risk for his tyres. In the background, a Pierrot seems in trouble with his bicycle and is about to fall, after puncturing his tyres. This poster by Léo Hindre no doubt makes an allusion to a play by Paul Marguerite, running in Paris some years before in the style of pantomime theatre revival: "Pierrot, his wife's killer". In this case, is Bibendum saving the life of the beautiful Columbine?

France, 1911
"Michelin bicycle tyres
The best, the least expensive".
Language: French
Illustration: Hindre
600 x 800mm

Businessmen and sponsors

This poster reveals a way of thinking that was very much in vogue in advertising at the turn of the century. The industrialists and businessmen commissioned their promotional posters directly from the artists of their choice. Most of the time, the artists were given a free hand and it was only when the commissioned work was finished that the patrons passed judgement. This was probably the case for this poster by Hindre, but also for all those from the "classic" period of approximately 1898 to 1920. Michelin's campaigns began at André Michelin's initiative.

The advent of "heavier than air"

This poster with its very classic composition shows an aircraft flying over a part of the French city of Clermont-Ferrand, with its majestic cathedral, the Puy de Dôme in the background. In the foreground, the entrance to Michelin's Carmes factory. It is possible to see Bibendum's "Coup de la Semelle" on the façade. The event referred to with this lithograph is important, in that it contributed significantly to the prestige of the Michelin name and its popularity. On 7 March 1908, the Michelin brothers proposed participating in the rise of aviation by offering a prize of 100 000 Francs (or 5 000 guineas) to he who would "leave from Paris and come to rest gently on the summit of the Puy de Dôme, in less than 6 hours and with a passenger". On 7 March 1911, exactly three years after the creation of the prize, Eugène Renaux and his partner Albert Farman succeeded in the exploit with a time of five hours, ten minutes and forty-six seconds.

France, 1911
"Renaux flying over Clermont-Ferrand before landing on the Puy de Dôme, 7 March 1911".
Language: French
Event-related promotional poster: Michelin Grand Prix for Aviation
Illustration: Gamy
370 x 750mm

Is our future in art or in the air?

Over a million copies of the brochure "Our future is in the air" were distributed by the Michelin brothers in 1912. It had an unusual influence. Pablo Picasso drew inspiration from it to paint "The Scallop Shell: Our Future is in the Air", in oil and varnish on an oval-shaped canvas.

The time of the "marvellous mad drivers"

So that the tyre would dominate over rail, which was then at its height, Michelin commissioned a poster from Montaut announcing the (theoretical) victory of the motor-car over the rail-car. This was a promotional argument based not on the reality of a race, but on audaciously listing and comparing the kilometres covered by motor vehicles for certain specific destinations and their corresponding train schedules. The result, one of the most dynamic posters by the illustrator and one which made all the "marvellous mad drivers" of the period, wealthy and reasonably breakneck, dream. It is interesting to be able to compare the three versions reproduced here:
- the French one shows an honest country fellow, so frightened by the passage of the motor-car, that he goes halfway out of the poster's frame (it took daring to do this in 1905!),
- the Italian one, much closer to Montaut's coloured sketch, includes all the information
- the English version, much more reserved, is content to announce the name at the top and a modest title "the rail vanquished by Michelin tyres", perhaps because they are continental comparisons which are cited as proof (and not reproduced).
It should be noted that Bibendum's character never inspired Montaut's brush, which probably explains the Michelin Man's absence from these posters.

IL PNEUMATICO MICHELIN HA VINTO LA STRADA FERRATA

IL PNEUMATICO MICHELIN HA VINTO LA STRADA FERRATA

CIRCUITO DELLE ARDENNE._ HEATH percorse 600 chilometri in 6 ore 30'
COPPA FLORIO._ BRESCIA MATTEO CEIRANO compiva 300 chilometri in 2 ore 40' 48"
COPPA VANDERBILT._ LANCIA percorse 300 chilometri in 2 ore 39'
L'EXPRESSO Parigi-Calais, il treno piu rapido { 300 chilometri in 3 ore 20
del mondo, percorse { 600 chilometri in 6 ore 50 (andate e ritorno)

LE PNEU MICHELIN A VAINCU LE RAIL.

LE PNEU MICHELIN A VAINCU LE RAIL.

Heath - Circuit des Ardennes 1904 - 600 Kilom. en 6 h. 30
Hemery - Circuit des Ardennes 1905 - 600 Kilom. en 5 h. 58
Lancia - Coupe Vanderbilt 1905 - 300 Kilom. en 2 h. 59

L'express Paris-Calais,   (298 Kilom. en 3 h. 20
le train le plus rapide du monde... (600 Kilom. en 6 h. 50 (aller et retour)

Grand Hôtel de Paris, La Bourboule-les-Bains

Menu

1

Italy, 1905
"The Michelin tyre vanquishes the rail".
Language: Italian
800 x 1200mm

2

France, 1905
"The Michelin tyre vanquishes the rail".
Language: French
800 x 1200mm

3

Menu published in 1905 for the "Grand Hôtel de Paris, Bourboule-les Bains" on the occasion of the Coupe Gordon-Bennett "The Triumph of the Road" Bibendum (the Michelin tyre) leads Madame the Road to the height of her glory". Illustration: Montaut.

4

This sketch, which includes the 1905 poster, appeared on the back cover of "L'Illustration théâtrale", a supplement to the weekly magazine "L'Illustration" of 27 December 1913.

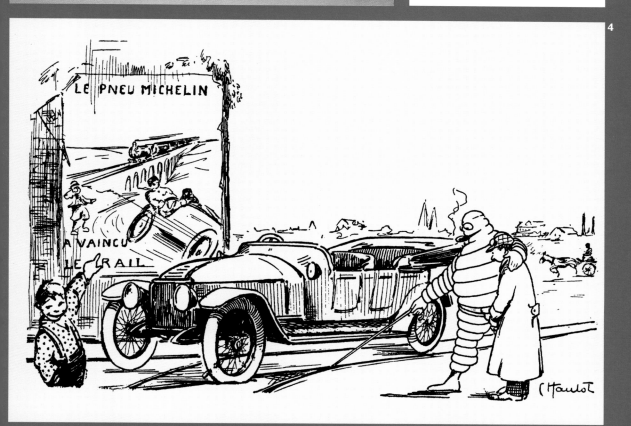

Ernest Montaut (1879-1936)

French painter, watercolourist and lithographer. Little is known of this artist who devoted his talents to the glory of locomotion: the motor-car, the aircraft, the blimp, the motor-boat... His lithographs, prized by collectors, represent various trophies, courses and raids as well as various names of automobiles. Montaut was also the author of a book entitled "Ten Years of Racing: 1897-1907". The collaboration of Montaut was not limited to this poster, as he also designed the ceramic tile panels celebrating the first victories of the Michelin brothers and the drivers of the cars fitted with the company's tyres. These ceramics now decorate offices of the Michelin Publicity Department in Paris and the famous Michelin House in Kensington, London.

Sir Bibendum, white knight

When the tyre is covered with metal studs, Bibendum dons a knight's armour to announce the news...and to affirm his invulnerability, to all of Great Britain. It is amusing to look at the fantasy coat-of-arms on "Sir Bibendum's" shield by his creator, the facetious O'Galop. It could be described as follows: quartered; gules, with spectacles; gules, three cigars with rings; vert, iron-shod tyre pierced by dagger; black, champagne glass with sharp-flavoured brew!...
It is of course, a pair of André Michelin's glasses, three of Bibendum's cigars, the "treaded" tyre with its reputation for invincibility, and the famous champagne glass full of shards, nails and broken glass, Bibendum's favourite "drink"...

1 ....
Great Britain, 1905
"Sir Bibendum, My strength is as the strength of ten Because my rubber's pure. (Adaptation of a citation of Tennyson) The Michelin Tyre Co. Ltd".
Language: English
Illustration: O'Galop
1500 x 2000mm

2

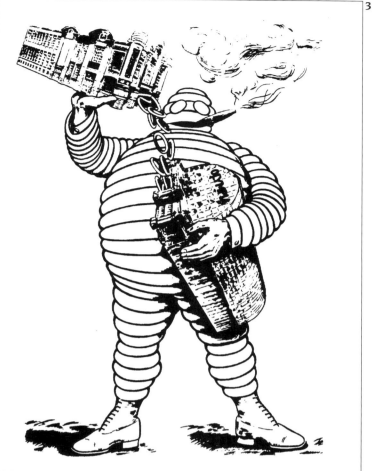

3

4

A long-lasting tread

The poster "The kick of the Michelin tread" is very much characteristic of its period, illustrating the aggression reigning in pneumatic tyre advertising at the beginning of the century. At the time there was no question of being gentle with the competition. Bibendum practises French boxing in answer to external attacks (notably the English Dunlop, supporter of English boxing). Dressed in exotic leopard-skin boxing briefs, he lets fly with an authoritative kick...to show the sole of his boot, the Michelin tread. This poster is a manifestation of O'Galop's remarkable mastery of graphic art. His drawing makes much of both the character's and the tyre's dynamism and flexibility. This is probably one of the best advertising posters of the period.

1 ....

France, 1905
Language: French
Illustration: O'Galop
1200 x 1600mm

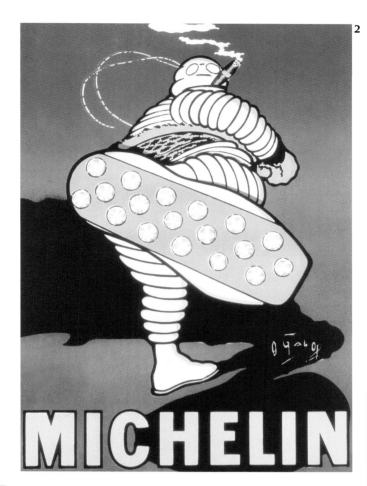

MICHELIN

MICHELIN-GLEITSCHUTZ
MIT GEPANZERTER DOPPELSOHLE

DEUTSCHE MICHELIN · PNEUMATIK
AKTIENGESELLSCHAFT
FRANKFURT A·M·

MICHELIN
"SEMELLE" NON-SKID

ON
DETACHABLE RIM

(1) It _is_ a non-skid.
(2) The tread is an integral part of the cover.
(3) It is virtually puncture proof.
(4) It is as supple as an ordinary plain tread cover.
(5) It is suitable for all weathers, and all
    kinds of road surfaces.

2

France, 1902
"The kick of the Michelin tread"
Product presented: "Semelle" tyre
1200 x 1600mm

The text has disappeared from this poster,
probably meant for the English market; the
area is left entirely for the product to speak
for itself.

3

Germany, 1906
"Anti-skid Michelin tyre
with reinforced double tread"
Language: German
490 x 890mm

Germany was outside Franco/British rivalry
and their two styles of boxing. This country
discovered the Michelin Semelle tyre by a
totally different style of graphic art, from
which Bibendum is absent.

4

Circa 1905
The Michelin Paris branch at 97 Boulevard
Péreire. Two "kick of the Michelin tread"
tile panels on the corner of the building
show how important this poster was in
Michelin's advertising at the time.

5

United Kingdom, 1905
"Michelin "Semelle" non-skid"
Language: English

**"Thou shalt adopt our
"Semelle" tyre"**

Tyres had a lot to cope with on the
roads at the time; not only were they
often in very poor condition, above all
there were numerous nails scattered
everywhere by badly shod horses.
Michelin had the imagination to give its
tyres a band of cured leather reinforced
with a series of extra-strong steel studs.
This anti-skid measure, flexible and
resistant to punctures, a sort of
sculpturing before proper treads,
proved itself for many years.

Michelin victories by the dozen

Bibendum has loved competition ever since he was born. To prove the quality of his tyres and to enhance his reputation, he frequents the race tracks, throws himself fully into each race and takes off with a good number of victories at the finish line. Each year between 1900 and 1912 (the year of its first official withdrawal from competition) Michelin published a small poster to make its victories known. They were displayed at tyre distributors and in the most-frequented competition places.

France, 1905
"1905 Michelin Victories: Gordon Bennett Cup, Ardennes Circuit, Delhi-Bombay, Ostende Week, Brescia Meeting, Munich Week, Montreux Course".
Language: French
Event-related promotional poster
450 x 600mm

LES VICTOIRES DE MICHELIN
DANS L'ANNÉE 1905

COUPE GORDON BENNETT
CIRCUIT D'AUVERGNE
Le 1er THÉRY - Voiture Richard-Brasier
et les 4 premiers
étaient sur pneus "MICHELIN"

CIRCUIT DES ARDENNES
VOITURES
Le 1er HEMERY - Voiture Darracq
et les 5 premiers
étaient sur pneus "MICHELIN"
VOITURETTES
Le 1er WAGNER - Voiturette Darracq
était sur pneus "MICHELIN"

COURSE DE DEHLI BOMBAY
INDES
Le 1er SOREL - Voiture Dietrich
1er grand prix
était sur pneus "MICHELIN"

COUPE GORDON BENNETT
ÉLIMINATOIRES FRANÇAISES
Le 1er THÉRY - Voiture Richard Brasier
et les 14 premiers
étaient sur pneus "MICHELIN"

SEMAINE D'OSTENDE
CIRCUIT DU LITTORAL
1re Catégorie
Le 1er JAMAR - Voiture Germain
2e Catégorie
Le 1er VANDERSTEGEN - Voiture F.I.A.T.
étaient sur pneus "MICHELIN"

MEETING DE BRESCIA
COUPE FLORIO
Le 1er RAGGIO - Voiture Itala
et les 10 premiers
étaient sur pneus "MICHELIN"
COURSE DES 1000 KILes
L'équipe gagnante STUCCHI
était sur pneus MICHELIN

SEMAINE DE MUNICH
COURSE BLEICHROEDER
Le 1er HYERONIMUS - Voiture Mercédès
était sur pneus "MICHELIN"

COURSE DE MONTREUX
Le 1er Colonel de LOYS - Voiture La Buire
et les 4 premiers
étaient sur pneus "MICHELIN"

arrivée de Théry 1er

After having fitted a racing-car with pneumatic tyres for the first time in the world, for the Paris-Bordeaux-Paris race (1895), the Michelin brothers carried off their first victory on the French Côte d'Azur in 1897 (Marseille-Nice race) with a De Dion steam brake nicknamed "La Vaporeuse" ("Misty"). In 1899 the "Jamais contente" ("Never satisfied") electric vehicle, driven by Jenatzy and fitted with Michelin stretchable beaded tyres, breaks the 100km/hr barrier. This is the beginning of a fantastic period for motor-racing, a sport which contributes to establishing Michelin's European reputation. In 1905, for example, the sixth and last Gordon-Bennett Cup (Grand Prix Auvergne) saw Théry victorious on Michelin "Semelle" tyres.

2

Document:
French driver Théry driving in front of the grandstands on the Auvergne circuit. One will note the reminders of Michelin victories on the roof: the great capital-to-capital races such as Paris-Amsterdam-Paris; Paris-Berlin; Paris-Madrid; Paris-Vienna, etc. There is a series of "Michelin tyres drink up obstacles" posters in the background, on the barrier in front of the racegoers. These great international competitions raise an indescribable enthusiasm in the crowds. High society is also very interested, seeing very exciting entertainment in the races, an occasion to show themselves off to advantage and be with other people "of quality", while giving free rein to each person's chauvinism. These spectators and enthusiasts are essentially the customers for motor-cars - and tyres - up to 1914.

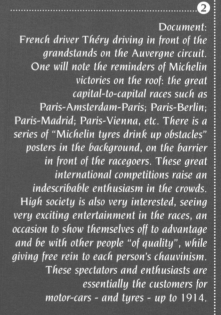

3

COUPE GORDON BENNETT (1905). — Circuit Michelin. — Pont de Champrader et Virage. — LL.

3

Document:
Gordon Bennett Cup (1905), a "Michelin tyre drinks up obstacles" poster on the Champrade bridge near Clermont-Ferrand.

A healthy mind in a healthy body

Gymnastics is one of the great passions of the average European at the beginning of the century, as is shown by Pierre de Coubertin's interest in bringing back the Olympic Games. Bibendum, very much part of his period, takes advantage of the introduction of his Exerciser onto the market to promote his tyres. On the poster (2), H. Delaspre gives a very fashionable Bibendum (top hat and cane) a resolutely detached air while he sees to three villains which have come to attack him. The idea of the "kick of the Michelin tread", which would appear three years later, was already in the air. Note the curves of the border, very much in the Art Nouveau style.
The other poster plays on the pseudo-scientific appeal by having an erudite curator saying, "According to my hypothesis, Venus of Milo used the Michelin Exerciser!"

1 ....

France, 1902
"There is no doubt that Venus of Milo used the Michelin Exerciser with her arms!"
340 x 480mm

2

France, 1902
"The Michelin Man
defies all attacks
because he uses
the Michelin Exerciser".
Language: French
Illustration: Delaspre
340 x 480mm

The exercise of the Exerciser

This body-building device, the first model dating from 1901, is a product made of rubber. At this time a certain Mr. Sandow made his fortune with a very similar apparatus. The instructions which came with Michelin's product explained: "The Michelin Exerciser is the best and the least expensive of home gymnastics equipment. It makes it possible for sports enthusiasts to stay in trim out of season. It also allows those leading a sedentary life to take healthy exercise without losing time, which will give them back their appetite and their sleep".

"Nunc est Bibendum", the new era of the pneumatic tyre

This poster, "Nunc est Bibendum" (very loosely: "Now let's drink"), is certainly the most famous poster published by Michelin. It is also the one which carries the greatest emotion. How can you not be amazed at the birth of Bibendum, this incredible "Michelin Man" who has become the most popular promotional character in the world?
What a fabulous brain-child, this subtle mix of chance and successive intuitions, spread over five years. So, let us leave the task of telling this extraordinary story in the care of Bibendum himself: "You will permit me first to consider as historic this sentence which made my fortune and to which I owe my fortune and my very existence: "The tyre drinks up obstacles". This illustrious and pithy expression has often caused others to ask me who used it for the first time.
Well, naturally, it was my papa André Michelin!
Where? At the French Society of Civil Engineers, during a conference which took place in February 1893. By then, Michelin had done its utmost for two or three years to manufacture detachable bicycle tyres. In 1891 its first battle ended in a resounding victory:

Charles Terront, thanks to his detachable Michelin tyres, won the famous Paris-Brest-Paris race, beating the greatly favoured Jiel-Laval, who rode on non-detachable tyres.
But the idea of the detachable tyre still met with incredulity. Therefore it had to be defended and explained. André Michelin, at a conference, showed the progress cycling had made owing to the pneumatic tyre and he gave them a glimpse of the remarkable boost it was going to give the bicycle. Then he concluded his demonstration by these words, which perfectly summarised his thoughts: "The tyre drinks up obstacles".
From his listeners' approbation, he felt that this improvised assertion was the right one.
In 1894 the Michelin brothers visited their distributor's stand at the Lyon Exhibition.
Stopping in front of a pile of tyres wrapped in a special white paper, Edouard said to André: "Good heavens, if it had arms and legs, it would make a man!"
In April 1898 a graphic artist showed André Michelin a caricature offered to and refused by a Munich brewery, representing a "colossal" man brandishing an enormous tankard while crying "Nunc est bibendum".
That day, André Michelin had one of his strokes of genius.

He asked O'Galop to bring together the "man" in the pile of tyres, to replace the tankard with a champagne glass full of glass shards and various nails and to complete the Latin motto with a "free" translation.
It only took an evening and the "adapted" son that I am was born to live under the great sun of Publicity. I existed, but I was not yet baptised. My godfather was Théry, who would drive the Richard-Brasier to glorious victories in the latter Gordon-Bennett races.
"Bibendum", this Latin word, incomprehensible and pleasant-sounding, pleased him. Seeing André Michelin in the distance one day, he cried, "Here's Bibendum! Long live Bibendum!" And Bibendum thus became a synonym for Michelin, and, at the same time, the name of your servant".
(L'Illustration, 5 June 1920)

Homage to O'Galop

But it was not enough to create the character. He had to live, develop a personality, go out into the world, be given the best education. O'Galop would take this task in hand.
This French graphic artist of the Humoristic School and water-colourist collaborated with André Michelin for over ten years creating dozens of postcards and several posters, without forgetting France's famous coloured picture prints from Epinal and a good hundred or so advertisements in the press. Born Marius Rossillon (born Lyon - 1867, died Carsac - 1946) he set himself on a new course in the cinema after 1918 and produced over twenty animated cartoons which were distributed by Pathé Baby in the 1930s.

PNEUMATIQUES MICHELIN
Clermont-Ferrand
Nº 421.

NUNC est bibendum. c'est à

VOTRE SANTÉ LE PNEU Michelin BOIT L'OBSTACLE!

LA GRÈVE DES COCHERS DE FIACRE (d'après F. COPPÉE)
Cette histoire, Messieurs les juges, sera brève.
Voilà. Les bons cochers de fiacre s'étaient mis en grève
C'était leur droit, chacun d'eux était las du plein,
Comme le client, ils voulaient du MICHELIN.

Nº 382
PNEUMATIQUES MICHELIN
Clermont-Ferrand

L'ALCOOLISME

LE PNEU MICHELIN BOIT L'OBSTACLE

LE PNEU X : Est-ce qu'ils ne feraient pas mieux de supprimer les caniveaux,
les clous....
LE PNEU Y : Les ornières.....
LE PNEU X : Les culs....
LE PNEU Y : de bouteilles!!!
BIBENDUM : Moi, je m'en f...! je bois l'obstacle!

"Indoor" posters

Certain posters bore the words: "Poster to be placed indoors only". This instruction was put into effect from the day when, on a poster proclaiming "The Michelin tyre drinks up obstacles", another tyre manufacturer wrote the pernicious line: "And it bursts with them". After this incident, the company's posters were designed to be placed inside distributors' windows or in garages. Apart from the copies meant for the large billboard networks, it would seem that the decision still holds, virtually a century later.

❺
....
France, 1904
Michelin tyre glue
and accessories on the table
Language: French
Corporate poster
Illustration: O'Galop
1200 x 1600mm

❻
....
France, 1912
Air cylinder
1200 x 1600mm

❼
....
France, 1913
Numerous Michelin accessories on the table
1200 x 1600mm

❽
....
France, April 1898
"Nunc est Bibendum, that is to say,
your good health!
The Michelin tyre drinks up obstacles".
Language: French
Corporate poster
Bibendum lifts his champagne glass
"Your good health"
Illustration: O'Galop
1200 x 1600mm

The various editions of the poster: "Nunc est Bibendum"

Each of these versions has its peculiarities. Bibendum smokes or does not, his spectacles change shape, his competitors X and Y (caricatures of the Dunlop and Continental company chiefs of the period) are more or less deflated, in fact have virtually disappeared in some cases. In certain versions, the original colours are beiges and reds; others are a black background grading into green tones, blues or yellows, etc.

1832
1998

From the elastic ball...
to the round ball

Whatever the vehicle, the wheel turns and always comes back to its starting point. And so it is with this long voyage through the bustling life of Bibendum and Michelin's corporate image through graphic art - which brings us back, naturally, to today!

Other times, other competitions. Bibendum is in energetic form to blow out the hundred candles on his cake, still hale and hearty, being the trained sports enthusiast that he is. Is he not undeniably an official sponsor of the 1998 World Cup for football?

Just a little time with his designers for some slight weight-reduction treatment and here he is ready to take off again, younger and slimmer than ever, ready to "drink up obstacles" in a new century of adventures...

Go for it,
Bibendum!

France, December 1997
Michelin, Official Tyre
for the World Cup
Poster: Michelin Paris Studio
Language: Exists in French,
English, Spanish
600 x 800mm

....

APPENDICES

The printers: *Often forgotten, they deserve no less attention than the illustrators. For the designers to conceive and make a graphic success of their posters, the care given to the printing of them is of vital importance.*

Some of Michelin's poster printers over the last hundred years:
Bastard-Fouqueray, Paris - Beaudet, Paris - Bedos et Cie, Paris - Chaix, Paris - Cornille et Serre, Paris - Courbet, Paris - Danjaq SA, London - Debladis, Paris - Draeger, Paris - Gagnier, Auxerre - Goossens, Brussels - Imprimerie des Arts et Industries, Les Reproductions Industrielles, Paris - Lucien Serre, Paris - Mausse Delhalle, Paris - Nerson et Schill, Paris - Revon, Paris - Waterlow & Sons, London - etc.

When O'Galop signed the Michelin petition demanding that French roads be systematically numbered (October 1912) he drew this rapid sketch of Bibendum (Archives Nationales).

....

ACKNOWLEDGEMENTS

Our gratitude to: Alain Arnaud, Paul Bonnetain, Daniel Bordet, Didier Derbal, Michel François, Pierre Dupasquier, Didier Hée, Gonzague de Jarnac, Pierre Métayer, Michel Moulin, Paul Niblett, Jacques Pouillous, Annick Rouaud, Louis Saugues, Elizabeth Sevo, Anne-Sophie Simonet, Alain Sonolet, the daily La Montagne-Centre-France, the weekly "La vie du Collectionneur", the BDDP agency

Special thanks to the graphic artists of the Michelin Paris Studio: Robert Cuzin, Bernadette Drouillot, Raymonde Faimali, Yves Le Gal, Michel Guillot, Claude Moreno, Gérard Radegonde, Jean-Claude Salbert as well as to the photographers and public relations companies which lend their know-how and talent to aid Michelin's communications. Without them, this work would not have existed.

Documents: Michelin archives

Manufacture Française des Pneumatiques Michelin
Place des Carmes-Déchaux - 63000 Clermont-Ferrand (France)
© Michelin et Cie, Propriétaires-Éditeurs 1998
Dépot légal : septembre 1998 - ISBN 2-06-149901-5

Imprimé en France en juillet 1998
sur les presses de l'Agence Le Sanglier - Charleville-Mézières
Relieur N.R.I. - Auxerre